Luscious Low-Fat Favorites

Now, you can experience the pleasure of eating the foods you love, while trimming fat and calories from your diet at the same time. With pride, Tupperware® brings you this special collection of deliciously low-fat recipes. Starting with the Vegetable Lasagna Rolls shown on the cover, sample each savory creation in this book. You'll be delightfully surprised how easy—and enjoyable—eating low-fat really can be.

Produced by Meredith Publishing Services, 1912 Grand Avenue, Des Moines, IA 50309-3379

This seal assures you that every recipe in **Luscious Low-Fat Favorites** has been tested in the *Better Homes and Gardens*® Test Kitchen. This means that each recipe is practical and reliable, and meets high standards of taste appeal.

All microwave recipes were tested in a variety of high-wattage microwave ovens. Cooking times are approximate since microwave ovens vary by manufacturer.

Contents

3

Eating the Low-Fat Way

Everywhere you turn today, experts are recommending that you reduce the amount of fat in your diet. That recommendation is easy to make but not always to follow. Here's information that will help.

What Does "Low-Fat" Really Mean?

Health experts recommend that no more than 30 percent of your calorie intake come from fat—and you'll be glad to know that every recipe in this book meets this guideline. But that doesn't mean you have to avoid higher-fat foods completely. Just enjoy them in moderation. Your goal should be to balance your consumption of foods high and low in fat so your average—over a period of a week, for instance—stays within the 30 percent guideline.

Calculating a Food's Fat Percentage

If you don't know the fat percentage of a food, it's easy to calculate. First find the number of grams of fat and the number of calories in a single serving by checking the charts on pages 88–93 or a calorie handbook. For packaged foods, look at the nutrition label. Then, make this three-step calculation:
• Multiply the grams of fat by 9—the calories each gram of fat contains.
• Divide this number by the total number of calories per serving.
• Finally, multiply this result by 100. The result is the percentage of calories from fat.

Shop Smart

Low-fat cooking really starts at the supermarket. You can trim a lot of fat from your diet simply by learning to select low-fat ingredients. In your store's meat section, for instance, look for lean meat cuts such as beef top round and pork tenderloin. Poultry and fish make excellent low-fat choices, too, though some fish such as salmon is high in fat and should be eaten only occasionally.

With milk, skim or 1 percent milk is your best choice. Look for cheese with less than 6 grams of fat per ounce.

Most fruits and vegetables, both fresh and frozen, are low in fat and calories, contain no cholesterol, and are rich in vitamins and minerals. As long as you serve them without high-fat accompaniments, such as butter, you can eat all the fruits and vegetables you like.

Most breads—including white and whole wheat bread, bagels, and English muffins—are also low in fat. Pass up croissants, butter rolls, sweet rolls, Danish pastry, and doughnuts, however.

To round out meals without adding much fat, serve plenty of cereals, pasta, and rice.

Cooking Tips

Trim all visible fat from meat before cooking. For ground meat, drain off the fat after cooking, and for poultry, avoid eating the skin.

Broiling and poaching and roasting on a rack are good low-fat cooking methods. Avoid deep-fat frying.

When sautéing, use a nonstick skillet and nonstick spray coating. If you do need to add a little cooking oil, choose a polyunsaturated or monounsaturated variety.

When a favorite recipe calls for cooking vegetables in margarine, butter, or oil, cook them in a little water instead. Once the vegetables are tender, just drain them and continue as the recipe directs.

One final tip: Throughout the book are many suggestions for cutting fat from your diet. If you incorporate them often into your new lifestyle, the result will be a healthier you.

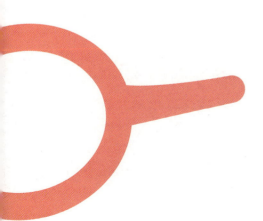

Nutrition Calculations

Each recipe in this book lists the nutrition values for one serving. Use these values to keep track of what you eat. Here's additional information about how we made our analyses.

When a recipe gives a choice of ingredients (such as chicken or beef broth), we used the first choice for our analysis.

Ingredients listed in the recipe as optional weren't included in our calculations.

We rounded all values to the nearest whole number.

Snacks and Appetizers

Snacks and appetizers always have been considered "extras"—and on a low-fat diet, they were forbidden extras. No more! Just stick to our suggested serving sizes, and you can snack away on one or two of these tasty tidbits everyday!

Fiesta Shrimp Appetizer
(See recipe, page 17.)

Layered Bean Dip

Per serving:
97 cal. (17% from fat), 5 g pro., 15 g carbo., 2 g fat,
2 mg cholesterol, 2 g dietary fiber, 282 mg sodium.

Preparation time:
25 minutes

Chilling time:
4 hours

Using homemade Tortilla Crisps instead of commercial corn chips helps trim fat and calories.

1   15-ounce can pinto or red kidney beans, drained

¼   cup salsa

1   4-ounce can diced green chili peppers, drained

4   ounces bottled roasted red bell pepper, drained and chopped (about ½ cup), or one 4-ounce jar pimiento, drained and chopped

1   cup low-fat cottage cheese

1   cup chopped tomato

¼   cup shredded low-fat cheddar cheese

Tortilla Crisps (see recipe at right) or assorted raw vegetable dippers

• Place beans and salsa in a blender container or food processor bowl. Cover and blend or process until smooth. Spread mixture evenly in a 9-inch pie plate. Sprinkle with green chili peppers and roasted red pepper or pimiento.

• Wash blender container or food processor bowl. Place cottage cheese in the blender container or food processor bowl. Cover and blend or process until smooth. Then, carefully spread cottage cheese on top of bean mixture in pie plate. Cover and chill for at least 4 hours before serving.

• Before serving, sprinkle tomato and cheddar cheese on top of cottage-cheese layer. Serve with Tortilla Crisps or assorted vegetable dippers. Makes 18 servings (4 crisps and ¼ cup dip per serving).

Tortilla Crisps: Cut twelve 6-inch *flour* or *corn tortillas* into 6 wedges each. Place wedges in a single layer on an ungreased baking sheet. Bake in a 350° oven for 5 to 10 minutes or until crisp.

Say Cheese!

A wide variety of lower-fat and nonfat cheeses have become available, making it much easier to use cheese and yet keep an eye on fat. For your next party, serve a selection of the following cheeses with low-fat crackers, melba toast, split and toasted small bagels, apple slices, and/or pear wedges:

Lower-fat natural cheeses, such as cheddar, Swiss, and Monterey Jack, are 50 to 75 percent lower in fat than regular natural cheeses but are not imitation cheeses. Lower-fat mozzarella cheese is labeled "part-skim."

Lower-fat flavored process cheese products are available in several flavors, including American, cheddar, and Swiss.

Nonfat process cheese products contain no fat. American-flavor is the most commonly available of these products.

Caramel Corn

Per serving:
139 cal. (26% from fat), 1 g pro., 26 g carbo., 4 g fat,
0 mg cholesterol, 1 g dietary fiber, 74 mg sodium.

Preparation time:
15 minutes

Cooking time:
5 minutes

Baking time:
20 minutes

Making 9 cups of popped popcorn without fat is easy when you use an air popper or a microwave popcorn popper. You'll need ½ cup (3 ounces) of unpopped popcorn.

9 cups popped popcorn (using no oil)

⅔ cup packed brown sugar

⅓ cup light corn syrup

3 tablespoons margarine

½ teaspoon vanilla

¼ teaspoon baking soda

- Remove all unpopped kernels from the popped popcorn. Put popcorn in a 17x12x2-inch baking pan.

- Combine the brown sugar, corn syrup, and margarine in a 1½-quart saucepan. Cook and stir over medium heat until margarine melts and mixture boils. Reduce heat to medium-low. Cook, without stirring, 5 minutes more. Remove from heat. Stir in vanilla and baking soda. Pour syrup mixture over popcorn in baking pan and gently stir to coat.

- Bake in a 300° oven for 15 minutes; stir. Bake 5 minutes more. Transfer popcorn mixture to a large piece of foil; cool completely. Break into clusters. Store tightly covered. Makes 9 (1-cup) servings.

Sweet-and-Spicy Popcorn

Per serving:
49 cal. (9% from fat), 1 g pro., 11 g carbo., 1 g fat,
0 mg cholesterol, 1 g dietary fiber, 0 mg sodium.

Preparation time:
10 minutes

Baking time:
15 minutes

Store this flavorful snack in the Tupperware® 6-cup Classic Sheer® Wonderlier® bowl.

6 cups popped popcorn (using no oil)

Nonstick spray coating

2 tablespoons sugar

2 teaspoons water

¼ teaspoon ground cinnamon

⅛ teaspoon ground nutmeg

⅛ teaspoon ground ginger

- Remove all unpopped kernels from the popped popcorn. Spray a cold 13x9x2-inch baking pan with nonstick spray coating. Place popcorn in the baking pan.

- Stir together sugar, water, cinnamon, nutmeg, and ginger in a small mixing bowl. Add spice mixture to popcorn in baking pan. Toss popcorn until coated. Bake in a 350° oven for 15 minutes, stirring once or twice.

- Transfer popcorn mixture to a large piece of foil; cool completely. Store popcorn mixture tightly covered. Makes 6 (1-cup) servings.

*Fancy Finger
Sandwiches*

Oven-Fried Vegetables

Per serving:
46 cal. (22% from fat), 2 g pro., 7 g carbo., 1 g fat,
1 mg cholesterol, 1 g dietary fiber, 190 mg sodium.

Preparation time:
15 minutes

Baking time:
9 minutes

With this trimmed-down recipe, you can have the flavor of regular deep-fried vegetables without all the fat and calories. The secret is the oven-frying with nonstick spray coating.

Nonstick spray coating

¼ cup fine dry bread crumbs

1 tablespoon grated Parmesan cheese

⅛ teaspoon paprika

2 cups ¼-inch-thick zucchini slices, onion rings, or cauliflower flowerets

2 tablespoons nonfat Italian salad dressing

- Spray a cold baking sheet with nonstick spray coating. Set aside.

- Stir together bread crumbs, Parmesan cheese, and paprika in a 9-inch pie plate until well mixed.

- Place zucchini, onion rings, or cauliflower in a medium mixing bowl. Drizzle vegetables with salad dressing; toss until coated. Then roll vegetables in crumb mixture until coated. Place the coated vegetables in a single layer on the prepared baking sheet.

- Bake vegetables in a 450° oven for 9 to 11 minutes or until golden. Makes 4 (½-cup) servings.

Fancy Finger Sandwiches

Per serving (one sandwich topped with ham and chives):
61 cal. (30% from fat), 3 g pro., 8 g carbo., 2 g fat,
7 mg cholesterol, 1 g dietary fiber, 218 mg sodium.

Preparation time:
20 minutes

Create this inviting assortment of open-face sandwiches for a special party. Guests will love them and will never guess they're low-fat.

12 slices firm-textured rye or marbled rye bread

½ of an 8-ounce container light cream cheese product

2 teaspoons Dijon-style mustard

4 very thin slices (1 ounce total) fully cooked ham, turkey-ham, or smoked salmon, or 1 ounce tiny cooked shrimp*

Assorted vegetables: cherry tomato slices, radish slices, asparagus spear tips, cucumber slices, and/or green onion slices

Fresh dill or parsley sprigs or snipped chives

- Using a sharp knife or cookie cutters, cut bread slices into 2- to 3-inch-wide shapes (circles, triangles, or squares).

- Combine cream cheese product and Dijon-style mustard in a small mixing bowl. Thinly spread some of the cream cheese mixture on the bread cutouts.

- Cut slices of meat into wedges, rounds, or strips (about 2x1-inch pieces). If using salmon, cut into slivers. Arrange pieces of meat, fish, or shrimp on bread cutouts. Pipe remaining cream cheese mixture around edges. Top with desired vegetables. Garnish with dill or parsley sprigs or chives. Makes about 20 appetizers.

*To satisfy a variety of different tastes among party-goers, serve a combination of these toppers.

Salsa and Homemade Tortilla Chips

Per serving:
94 cal. (18% from fat), 3 g pro., 17 g carbo., 2 g fat,
0 mg cholesterol, 1 g dietary fiber, 258 mg sodium.

Preparation time:
20 minutes

Chilling time:
4 hours

Baking time:
20 minutes

A serving of this recipe has 45 percent fewer calories, 85 percent less fat, and 60 percent less sodium than a 1-ounce serving of purchased tortilla chips and 2 tablespoons of bottled salsa.

1   cup finely chopped peeled tomato

½   cup tomato sauce

1   4-ounce can diced green chili peppers, drained

¼   cup finely chopped green pepper

¼   cup sliced green onions

2   tablespoons lemon juice

1   to 2 tablespoons snipped cilantro or parsley

1   clove garlic, minced

⅛   teaspoon ground black pepper

Bottled hot pepper sauce (optional)

Homemade Tortilla Chips (see recipe at right)

Fresh cilantro (optional)

• Stir together the tomato, tomato sauce, chili peppers, green pepper, green onions, lemon juice, snipped cilantro or parsley, garlic, ground pepper, and, if desired, *several dashes* hot pepper sauce in a mixing bowl. Place about *half* of the tomato mixture in a blender container or food processor bowl. Cover and blend or process until smooth. Return blended mixture to the mixing bowl with the unblended tomato mixture; stir to mix well.

• Cover and chill at least 4 hours before serving, stirring occasionally. (May be stored in the refrigerator for up to 1 week.) Serve with Homemade Tortilla Chips. If desired, garnish with a sprig of cilantro. Makes 16 servings (6 chips and 2 tablespoons salsa per serving).

Homemade Tortilla Chips: Cut twelve 8-inch *flour tortillas* into 8 wedges each. Spread *half* of the wedges in a 15x10x1-inch baking pan. Bake in a 375° oven for 10 to 15 minutes or until dry and crisp, gently tossing once. Repeat with remaining chips. Cool completely. Store chips in a sealed Tupperware® brand container at room temperature for up to 4 days, or in the freezer for up to 3 weeks. Makes 96 chips (about 9 ounces).

Slim Snacks

Keep these fat-wise snacks handy for those times when the urge to nibble strikes:

1½ cups fresh whole strawberries topped with 1 tablespoon of plain low-fat yogurt—1 gram fat and 74 calories

½ cup cubed papaya topped with a ¼-cup scoop of rainbow sherbet—1 gram fat and 93 calories

1 medium orange, sectioned and sprinkled with 1 tablespoon of coconut—2 grams fat and 83 calories

1 slice raisin bread spread with 2 teaspoons of light cream cheese—3 grams fat and 91 calories

25 thin pretzels (2¼ inches long)—0 gram fat and 48 calories

2 cups cauliflower flowerets drizzled with 1 tablespoon nonfat ranch salad dressing—0 gram fat and 66 calories

1 cup lower-calorie cranberry juice cocktail—0 gram fat and 44 calories

Crunchy Party Mix

Per serving:
138 cal. (18% from fat), 3 g pro., 26 g carbo., 3 g fat,
0 mg cholesterol, 1 g dietary fiber, 294 mg sodium.

Preparation time:
15 minutes

Baking time:
45 minutes

Stretching the cooking oil in this snack with the butter-flavored mix results in fewer calories and less fat. Look for the mix in the seasoning section of your supermarket.

¼ cup water

3 tablespoons Worcestershire sauce

2 tablespoons butter-flavored mix

2 tablespoons cooking oil

½ teaspoon garlic powder

½ teaspoon seasoned salt

Several drops bottled hot pepper sauce

Nonstick spray coating

5 cups crispy corn and rice cereal

5 cups bite-size wheat-square cereal

4 cups lower-sodium pretzels

3 cups oyster crackers

- Combine water, Worcestershire sauce, butter-flavored mix, cooking oil, garlic powder, seasoned salt, and hot pepper sauce in a saucepan; heat and stir until butter-flavored mix dissolves.

- Spray a large roasting pan with nonstick coating. Add cereals, pretzels, and oyster crackers. Add butter-flavored mixture and toss to coat.

- Bake mixture in a 300° oven for 45 minutes, stirring every 15 minutes. Spread mixture on foil to cool. Store in a sealed Tupperware® brand container. Makes 32 (½-cup) servings.

Curried Snack Mix

Per serving:
73 cal. (28% from fat), 1 g pro., 12 g carbo., 2 g fat,
0 mg cholesterol, 0 g dietary fiber, 152 mg sodium.

Preparation time:
10 minutes

Baking time:
20 minutes

If you enjoy spicy foods, add the higher level of curry powder.

3 plain rice cakes, broken into bite-size pieces

1 cup bite-size corn-square cereal or oyster crackers

¾ cup pretzel sticks, halved (1 ounce)

1 tablespoon margarine, melted

1 teaspoon Worcestershire sauce

½ to ¾ teaspoon curry powder

- Stir together broken rice cakes, the corn-square cereal or oyster crackers, and pretzel sticks in a 13x9x2-inch baking pan.

- Stir together the melted margarine, Worcestershire sauce, and desired amount of curry powder in a custard cup. Drizzle the margarine mixture over the cereal mixture. Toss the cereal mixture until coated.

- Bake in a 300° oven for 20 minutes, stirring twice. If desired, store the cooled snack mixture in a sealed Tupperware container. Makes 6 (½-cup) servings.

Cottage Cheese and Dill Dip

Yogurt Fruit Dip

Per serving:
66 cal. (8% from fat), 2 g pro., 14 g carbo., 1 g fat,
2 mg cholesterol, 1 g dietary fiber, 21 mg sodium.

Preparation time:
10 minutes

Use the Tupperware® Small Serving Center® container to serve this refreshing snack.

1   8-ounce carton plain low-fat yogurt

¼   cup apricot or peach preserves

⅛   teaspoon ground cinnamon

2   apples, pears, and/or peaches

- Stir together yogurt, apricot preserves, and cinnamon. Slice fruit; serve with dip. Makes 8 (2-tablespoon) servings of dip.

Cottage Cheese and Dill Dip

Per serving:
35 cal. (12% from fat), 5 g pro., 4 g carbo., 0 g fat,
1 mg cholesterol, 1 g dietary fiber, 126 mg sodium.

Preparation time:
15 minutes

Chilling time:
1 hour

Present this luscious low-fat dip in a red pepper shell and serve with fresh raw vegetables, including asparagus, cherry tomatoes, cucumber slices, mushroom slices, and radishes.

1   cup low-fat cottage cheese

2   tablespoons sliced green onion

2   tablespoons snipped fresh parsley

1   teaspoon dried dillweed

1   teaspoon Worcestershire sauce

⅛   teaspoon pepper

Dash garlic powder

Assorted raw vegetable dippers

- Place the cottage cheese, green onion, snipped parsley, dillweed, Worcestershire sauce, pepper, and garlic powder in a blender container or food processor bowl. Cover and blend or process until smooth. Chill, covered, for at least 1 hour before serving.

- Serve with an assortment of raw vegetable dippers. Makes 8 (2-tablespoon) servings of dip.

Salmon Spread and Pita Wedges

Per serving:
83 cal. (24% from fat), 6 g pro., 10 g carbo., 2 g fat,
10 mg cholesterol, 0 g dietary fiber, 260 mg sodium.

Preparation time:
20 minutes

Chilling time:
2 hours

Baking time:
2 minutes

Cut calories and fat by making your own crisp chips from pita bread rounds split in half. For an added twist, use whole wheat pita rounds.

1   6½-ounce can skinless, boneless salmon, drained and flaked

¼   cup finely chopped celery

2   tablespoons finely chopped green onion

2   tablespoons plain low-fat yogurt

1   tablespoon Dijon-style mustard

1½ teaspoons snipped fresh dill or ½ teaspoon dried dillweed

    Nonstick spray coating

2   6-inch pita bread rounds

4   lettuce leaves

● Combine salmon, celery, green onion, yogurt, mustard, and dill in a medium mixing bowl. Mix well. Spray a 1-cup mold or bowl or a 10-ounce custard cup with nonstick coating. Press salmon mixture into the mold, bowl, or custard cup. Cover and chill for 2 to 24 hours.

● For pita wedges, split each pita bread round horizontally so you have four rounds. Cut each round into 8 wedges. Arrange wedges on a baking sheet. Bake in a 450° oven for 2 to 3 minutes or until dry and crisp. Cool.

● Line a serving plate with lettuce leaves. Invert the mold, bowl, or custard cup onto the lettuce-lined plate. Lift and remove the mold, bowl, or custard cup. Serve salmon mixture with pita wedges. Makes 8 servings (4 pita wedges and about 2 tablespoons salmon spread per serving).

Oil Facts

Although you can't avoid oils completely when you cook, you can make sure the oils you use are the best for you. The healthiest type of oil is one that is low in saturated fat—either a polyunsaturated or a monounsaturated cooking oil. Corn, sunflower, soybean, peanut, safflower, and canola oils are all good examples.

One monounsaturated oil especially favored by health professionals is olive oil. It's recommended because it contains a higher percentage of monounsaturated fat than other vegetable oils. What's so important about monounsaturated fat? Some studies indicate that monounsaturated fats help some people lower their blood cholesterol levels.

In general, use oils sparingly, and keep in mind that a nonstick skillet and nonstick spray coating often can eliminate the need for adding fat. As you select recipes for cookies, cakes, breads, and other baked goods, look for those that use cooking oil and avoid those that use shortening or lard.

Fiesta Shrimp Appetizer

Per serving:
49 cal. (26% from fat), 3 g pro., 6 g carbo., 1 g fat,
21 mg cholesterol, 1 g dietary fiber, 133 mg sodium.

Preparation time:
20 minutes

Cooking time:
1 minute

Marinating time:
2 hours

If you can't find Anaheim peppers at your supermarket, substitute jalapeño peppers. Start with 2 tablespoons of seeded and chopped jalapeños, then add 1 to 2 tablespoons more if you want a really fiery appetizer.

1	pound large shrimp, peeled and deveined
½	teaspoon finely shredded lime peel
¼	cup lime juice
1	tablespoon olive oil
2	tablespoons finely chopped green onion
¼	cup chopped Anaheim peppers
1	to 2 tablespoons snipped fresh cilantro or parsley
2	cloves garlic, minced
½	teaspoon sugar
½	teaspoon salt
	Kale or lettuce leaves
2	medium papayas, peeled, seeded, and sliced

- Cook shrimp in boiling water for 1 to 3 minutes or until shrimp turn pink; drain. Rinse in a colander, such as the Tupperware® Large Strainer or Double Colander, under cold running water; drain. Place shrimp in the Tupperware Season-Serve® container or a shallow dish.

- For marinade, combine lime peel, lime juice, olive oil, green onion, chopped Anaheim peppers, the cilantro or parsley, garlic, sugar, salt, and ¼ teaspoon *pepper*. Pour marinade over shrimp. Apply seal to Season-Serve container or cover dish. Marinate in the refrigerator for 2 to 3 hours, inverting container or stirring several times to distribute the marinade.

- Just before serving, line serving tray with kale or lettuce leaves. Arrange papaya slices and marinated shrimp on top. Garnish with fresh cilantro, if desired. Serves 12.

Note: Pictured on pages 6–7 in the Tupperware® Watercolor Hors D'oeuvre set.

Stuffed Mushrooms

Per serving:
26 cal. (23% from fat), 2 g pro., 4 g carbo., 1 g fat,
1 mg cholesterol, 1 g dietary fiber, 75 mg sodium.

Preparation time:
20 minutes

Baking time:
10 minutes

Stuff these savory mushrooms ahead, chill, then pop them in the oven right before serving time. You may have to add a minute or two to the baking time because the mushrooms will be cold. Just bake them until the mushrooms are tender and the filling is heated through.

1	10-ounce package frozen chopped spinach
	Nonstick spray coating
1½	pounds large fresh mushrooms (about 20)
¼	cup chopped onion
2	cloves garlic, minced
¼	cup grated Parmesan cheese
¼	cup fine dry bread crumbs
¼	cup finely chopped pimiento
½	teaspoon dried basil, crushed
½	teaspoon dried oregano, crushed

- Thaw spinach, then drain well by squeezing out excess liquid. Meanwhile, spray a cold 15x10x1-inch baking pan with nonstick coating. Set baking pan aside.

- Remove stems from mushrooms. Set tops aside. Chop enough mushroom stems to make *2 cups*. Spray a cold 10-inch skillet with nonstick coating. Cook chopped mushroom stems, onion, and garlic in skillet until onion is tender but not browned. Add drained spinach. Cook over low heat until most of the liquid is evaporated.

- Stir Parmesan cheese, bread crumbs, pimiento, basil, oregano, ¼ teaspoon *salt*, and dash *pepper* into spinach mixture. Spoon mixture into mushroom tops.

- Place stuffed mushroom tops in the prepared baking pan. Bake in a 425° oven for 10 to 15 minutes or until mushrooms are tender. Makes about 20 servings.

Marinated Zucchini and Mushrooms

Toasted Zucchini Snacks

Per serving:
21 cal. (16% from fat), 1 g pro., 4 g carbo., 0 g fat,
1 mg cholesterol, 0 g dietary fiber, 143 mg sodium.

Preparation time:
30 minutes

Standing time:
1 hour

Baking time:
12 minutes

Here's a terrific idea for using zucchini. Its fresh flavor blends perfectly with the yogurt, green onion and Romano cheese in this irresistible snack

2   cups shredded zucchini

1   teaspoon salt

½   cup lower-calorie mayonnaise or salad dressing

½   cup plain low-fat yogurt

3   tablespoons grated Romano cheese or Parmesan cheese

4   green onions, thinly sliced

1   teaspoon Worcestershire sauce

1   clove garlic, minced

¼   teaspoon bottled hot pepper sauce

48 slices party rye bread

- Stir together zucchini and salt in a bowl. Let stand at room temperature for 1 hour. Drain zucchini. Rinse. Drain well, pressing out excess liquid.

- Combine drained zucchini, the mayonnaise or salad dressing, yogurt, Romano or Parmesan cheese, onions, Worcestershire sauce, garlic, and hot pepper sauce. Stir together well.

- Spread a *rounded teaspoon* of the zucchini mixture on *each* party rye bread slice. Place on a baking sheet. Bake in a 375° oven for 12 minutes. Serve immediately. Makes 48.

Marinated Zucchini and Mushrooms

Per serving:
12 cal. (27% from fat), 0 g pro., 2 g carbo., 0 g fat,
0 mg cholesterol, 0 g dietary fiber, 21 mg sodium.

Preparation time:
20 minutes

Marinating time:
8 hours

The Tupperware® Season-Serve® container is ideal for marinating these colorful vegetables in a lemon-tarragon dressing,

8   ounces whole fresh mushrooms (3 cups)

2   small zucchini and/or yellow summer squash, bias-sliced into ½-inch-thick slices (2 cups)

1   small red sweet pepper, cut into square pieces (½ cup)

¼   cup lemon juice

2   teaspoons olive oil or cooking oil

4   teaspoons sugar

1   clove garlic, minced

¼   teaspoon salt

¼   teaspoon dried tarragon or oregano, crushed

¼   teaspoon pepper

- Cut mushrooms in half, if desired. Place mushrooms, zucchini and/or yellow squash, and red pepper in the Tupperware® Season-Serve® container or a shallow dish.

- For marinade, stir together lemon juice, oil, sugar, garlic, salt, tarragon or oregano, and pepper in a small mixing bowl. Mix well.

- Pour marinade over vegetables. Apply seal or cover dish. Invert container or stir several times to distribute marinade. Marinate vegetables in the refrigerator for 8 hours or overnight, inverting container occasionally to distribute marinade.

- To serve, thread zucchini, red pepper pieces, and mushrooms on 4-inch skewers. Makes 18 appetizers.

Main Dishes

The surest way to slash the most fat from your diet is to choose your main dishes wisely. With this wide variety of low-fat fare, you can select from dozens of meat, poultry, fish, seafood, and meatless entrées. The hardest part may be deciding which one to try first!

Indonesian Pork Skewers
(See recipe, page 29.)

Stir-Fried Pepper Steak

Per serving:
333 cal. (18% from fat), 26 g pro., 42 g carbo., 6 g fat,
66 mg cholesterol, 3 g dietary fiber, 423 mg sodium.

Preparation time:
15 minutes

Cooking time:
15 minutes

Stir-frying is a method for cooking food quickly in just enough cooking oil to prevent sticking. We reduced the fat in this recipe by using nonstick spray coating instead of oil to stir-fry the vegetables.

12 ounces boneless beef sirloin steak, cut ½ to ¾ inch thick

½ cup water

2 tablespoons lower-sodium soy sauce or 1 tablespoon Worcestershire sauce

1 tablespoon cornstarch

½ teaspoon instant beef bouillon granules

Dash pepper

6 ounces fettuccine

Nonstick spray coating

1 clove garlic, minced

1 medium onion, cut into thin wedges (¾ cup)

1 medium green pepper, cut into 1-inch pieces (1 cup)

2 medium tomatoes, cut into thin wedges (2½ cups)

- Trim fat from beef. Partially freeze beef; thinly slice across the grain into bite-size strips.

- For sauce, stir together water, soy sauce or Worcestershire sauce, cornstarch, bouillon granules, and pepper in a small bowl. Set the mixture aside.

- Cook the fettuccine according to the package directions, *except* omit the cooking oil and salt. Drain well.

- Meanwhile, spray a cold wok or large skillet with nonstick coating. Preheat over medium heat. Add the garlic to the wok and stir-fry for 15 seconds. Add the onion and stir-fry for 1 minute.

- Add the green pepper and stir-fry about 2 minutes more or until the vegetables are crisp-tender. Remove vegetables from the wok.

- Add beef to the hot wok or skillet. (If necessary, add a little *cooking oil*.) Stir-fry for 2 to 3 minutes or to desired doneness. Push beef from the center of the wok. Stir the sauce. Add the sauce to the center of the wok. Cook and stir until thickened and bubbly.

- Return the cooked vegetables to the wok or skillet. Stir all ingredients together to coat with sauce. Cook and stir about 1 minute more or until heated through. Gently stir in the tomato wedges. Heat through. Serve immediately over hot cooked fettuccine. Makes 4 servings.

Beef Teriyaki Stir-Fry

Per serving:
363 cal. (20% from fat), 33 g pro., 38 g carbo., 8 g fat,
71 mg cholesterol, 1 g dietary fiber, 974 mg sodium.

Preparation time:
5 minutes

Cooking time:
20 minutes

Partially freezing the beef makes it easier to slice. For best results, freeze the beef 45 to 60 minutes. At this stage, you'll be able to cut even, thin slices perfect for stir-frying.

1 pound beef top round steak

1 tablespoon cooking oil

3 cups loose-pack frozen broccoli, French-style green beans, onions, and red peppers

⅓ cup teriyaki sauce

2 cups hot cooked rice

- Partially freeze beef; thinly slice across the grain into bite-size strips. Add oil to a wok or large skillet; heat over high heat.

- Stir-fry vegetables 3 to 4 minutes or until crisp-tender; remove from wok. Add *half* of the beef to hot oil. Stir-fry 2 to 3 minutes or to desired doneness; remove from wok. Repeat with remaining beef. Return all beef to wok.

- Stir in teriyaki sauce and vegetables. Cook and stir about 1 minute more or until heated through. Serve over hot cooked rice. Makes 4 servings.

Spiced Beef Roast

Per serving:
187 cal. (30% from fat), 29 g pro., 4 g carbo., 6 g fat,
82 mg cholesterol, 0 g dietary fiber, 176 mg sodium.

Preparation time:
10 minutes

Roasting time:
1¼ hours

Standing time:
15 minutes

The next time you're planning a dinner party, remember this flavorful roast. Team it with a crisp tossed salad dressed with lower-fat cucumber ranch dressing and cooked baby carrots seasoned with a little light margarine and dried dillweed.

¼ teaspoon fennel seed

¼ teaspoon mustard seed

¼ teaspoon whole black peppercorns

1 2- to 2½-pound boneless beef round rump roast

1 cup sliced fresh mushrooms

1 cup skim milk

1 tablespoon cornstarch

½ teaspoon instant beef bouillon granules

1 tablespoon Dijon-style mustard

1 teaspoon snipped chives

- Crush the fennel seed, mustard seed, and whole black peppercorns using a mortar and pestle. Set aside.

- Trim fat from roast. Place roast on rack in a shallow roasting pan. Rub seed mixture over top and sides of roast. Insert a meat thermometer in the center of the roast. Roast, uncovered, in a 325° oven for 1¼ to 1¾ hours or until the meat thermometer registers 150° to 170°. Remove roast from oven. Cover with foil and let stand for 15 minutes before carving.

- Meanwhile, for sauce, in a small saucepan cook mushrooms in a small amount of boiling water about 3 minutes or until tender. Drain. Stir together milk, cornstarch, and bouillon granules. Add milk mixture to the drained mushrooms. Cook and stir until thickened and bubbly. Cook and stir 2 minutes more. Stir in mustard and chives. Serve with roast. Makes 8 servings.

Swiss Steak

Per serving:
369 cal. (20% from fat), 32 g pro., 41 g carbo., 8 g fat,
82 mg cholesterol, 4 g dietary fiber, 515 mg sodium.

Preparation time:
25 minutes

Cooking time:
1¼ hours

This light version of Swiss Steak is perfect for a fat-conscious lifestyle. Trimming the fat from the beef and using nonstick spray coating helps keep the calories from fat below 30 percent.

12 ounces boneless beef round steak, cut ¾ inch thick

Nonstick spray coating

1 14½-ounce can lower-sodium tomatoes, cut up

1 cup sliced celery

1 cup sliced carrots

1 small onion, sliced and separated into rings

⅓ cup water

½ teaspoon dried thyme, crushed

1 cup long-grain rice

1 tablespoon cold water

2 teaspoons cornstarch

- Trim fat from steak. Cut into 4 serving-size pieces. Spray a cold 12-inch skillet with nonstick coating. Preheat skillet. Brown steak on both sides.

- Add *undrained* tomatoes, celery, carrots, onion, the ⅓ cup water, the thyme, and ⅛ teaspoon *pepper*. Bring to boiling; reduce heat. Simmer, covered, about 1¼ hours or until meat is tender. Remove meat from skillet; cover and keep warm.

- Meanwhile, cook rice according to the package directions, *except* omit the margarine or butter and salt. Keep warm.

- For sauce, mix the 1 tablespoon water and the cornstarch; stir into tomato mixture. Cook and stir until thickened and bubbly. Cook and stir 2 minutes more. Serve meat and sauce over hot cooked rice. Serves 4.

*Eye of Round with
Pineapple Salsa*

Eye of Round with Pineapple Salsa

Per serving:
182 cal. (26% from fat), 25 g pro., 8 g carbo., 5 g fat,
59 mg cholesterol, 1 g dietary fiber, 56 mg sodium.

**Preparation time:
25 minutes**

**Roasting time:
1¼ hours**

**Standing time:
15 minutes**

This tropical salsa is good not only with roast beef but with sandwiches, too. Store any leftovers in a Tupperware® brand container to seal in the freshness. Keep the salsa on hand to serve on burgers or with cold sliced beef, turkey, or chicken sandwiches.

1   2-pound beef eye of round roast

2   cups diced fresh pineapple

2   medium tomatoes, peeled, seeded, and chopped

¼   cup chopped red onion

1   jalapeño pepper, seeded and finely chopped

2   cloves garlic, minced

2   tablespoons snipped fresh cilantro

2   tablespoons lime or lemon juice

2   teaspoons sugar

- Trim fat from roast. Place roast on a rack in a shallow roasting pan. Insert a meat thermometer in the center of the roast. Roast, uncovered, in a 325° oven for 1¼ to 1¾ hours or until thermometer registers 140° for rare or for 1¾ to 2¼ hours or 160° for medium.

- Remove roast from oven. Cover with foil and let stand for 15 minutes before carving.

- To make pineapple salsa, place the pineapple, tomatoes, onion, jalapeño pepper, garlic, cilantro, lime or lemon juice, and sugar in a bowl. Stir together to combine. Serve with sliced roast. If desired, garnish with chili peppers and parsley. Makes 8 servings.

Note: To grill roast, arrange *medium* coals around a drip pan in a covered grill. Test for *medium-low* heat above the drip pan. Place roast on grill rack over drip pan but not over coals. Insert a meat thermometer. Lower the grill hood. Grill for 1 to 1¼ hours or until meat thermometer registers 140° for rare or for 1½ to 2 hours or 160° for medium.

Lean-Meat Strategies

Meat can be an excellent staple in your diet as long as you select cuts with your health in mind. If you enjoy beef, make sure you choose the leanest cuts. Beef tenderloin, top round, top loin, sirloin tip, eye of round, and sirloin are known as the "skinniest six." A 3-ounce cooked portion, trimmed of fat, has only 155 to 189 calories. Also remember that USDA "Select" grade beef is leaner than beef graded "Choice."

When it comes to pork, choose cuts with "loin" or "leg" in the name. Pork tenderloin is nearly as lean as skinless chicken breasts. Use it in a stir-fry or roast it as you would a beef roast. Ham, too, is very lean, with only about 30 calories and 1 gram of fat per ounce. Another lean pork choice is Canadian bacon. For lamb, the cuts with the least fat are those that come from the leg and loin.

Chili-Mac Skillet

Per serving:
321 cal. (26% from fat), 23 g pro., 37 g carbo., 9 g fat,
47 mg cholesterol, 8 g dietary fiber, 336 mg sodium.

Preparation time:
20 minutes

Cooking time:
20 minutes

The extra-lean ground beef and lower-fat Monterey Jack cheese add up to a lot less fat than in the classic version of this hearty pasta casserole. The lower-sodium beans, tomato sauce, and tomatoes add even more health appeal.

8	ounces 90% lean ground beef
½	cup chopped onion (1 medium)
1	15½-ounce can lower-sodium red kidney beans, drained
1	8-ounce can lower-sodium tomato sauce
½	of a 14½-ounce can lower-sodium tomatoes, cut up
½	cup elbow macaroni
½	cup chopped green pepper
¼	cup water
1	tablespoon chili powder
½	teaspoon garlic salt
¼	cup shredded lower-fat Monterey Jack or cheddar cheese (1 ounce)

- Cook ground beef and onion in a large skillet until meat is brown. Drain off fat.

- Stir in the kidney beans, tomato sauce, *undrained* tomatoes, *uncooked* macaroni, green pepper, water, chili powder, and garlic salt. Bring to boiling; reduce heat. Cover and simmer for 20 minutes, stirring often.

- Remove skillet from heat. Sprinkle meat mixture with shredded cheese. Cover and let stand for 2 minutes or until the cheese melts. Makes 4 servings.

Ground Meat Choices

Cooking with the leanest ground beef, turkey, and chicken available will help you cut back on fat and calories. Ground beef is sold with varying levels of fat—everything from 75 percent lean (25 percent fat) to 97 percent lean (3 percent fat). Whenever possible use 90 to 97 percent lean ground beef for dishes such as chili, tacos, and meat casseroles. In some parts of the country, you also can purchase a 95 percent lean beef product that has some of the fat replaced with water and plant-derived ingredients to maintain the moisture in cooked meat. When using this product, keep in mind that it will form softer burgers, meat loaves, and meatballs than those made with regular ground beef.

When it comes to ground turkey or chicken, it pays to take a second look at the label. Choose turkey and chicken that's at least 90 percent lean by weight. If there's no nutrition label, take a look at the meat. A lot of little white specks indicates that fat and skin were ground up with the meat, and the product probably is less than 90 percent lean. Sometimes you can purchase ground turkey breast, which generally is leaner than other ground turkey.

Stuffed Green Peppers

Per serving:
229 cal. (29% from fat), 15 g pro., 26 g carbo., 7 g fat, 42 mg cholesterol, 2 g dietary fiber, 71 mg sodium.

Preparation time:
15 minutes

Cooking time:
15 minutes

Baking time:
15 minutes

This fat-trimmed version of a classic recipe calls for 90 percent lean ground beef. If your supermarket carries even leaner ground beef, choose that and reduce the fat even further.

8	ounces 90% lean ground beef
⅓	cup chopped onion (1 small)
2	medium tomatoes, peeled and cut into wedges
½	cup long-grain rice
½	cup water
2	teaspoons Worcestershire sauce
1	teaspoon dried Italian seasoning, crushed
¼	teaspoon pepper
2	large green peppers
1	tablespoon grated Parmesan cheese (optional)

- Cook meat and onion in a large skillet until meat is brown and onion is tender. Drain off fat. Stir in the tomatoes, *uncooked* rice, water, Worcestershire sauce, Italian seasoning, and pepper. Bring to boiling; reduce heat. Cover and simmer for 15 to 18 minutes or until the rice is tender.

- Meanwhile, halve green peppers lengthwise and remove stem ends, seeds, and membranes. Immerse peppers into *boiling water* for 3 minutes. Place, cut side down, on paper towels to drain well.

- Spoon meat mixture into peppers. Place the peppers in a 2-quart square baking dish. Spoon any remaining meat mixture into baking dish.

- Bake, covered, in a 375° oven about 15 minutes or until heated through. Sprinkle peppers with Parmesan cheese, if desired. Makes 4 servings.

Beef-Barley Soup

Per serving:
196 cal. (24% from fat), 22 g pro., 17 g carbo., 5 g fat, 57 mg cholesterol, 4 g dietary fiber, 512 mg sodium.

Preparation time:
23 minutes

Cooking time:
1 hour

Keep some of this satisfying soup on hand for a quick meal on busy nights. Just cool the soup down in your refrigerator, ladle each serving into a Tupperware® Freezer Mates® Medium 1 container, and freeze it for up to two months.

1½	pounds boneless beef chuck
6	cups water
2	cups sliced celery
2	cups sliced fresh mushrooms
1	cup sliced carrots
1	cup chopped onion
1	teaspoon salt
1	teaspoon dried rosemary, crushed
½	teaspoon pepper
1	clove garlic, minced
1	6-ounce can tomato paste
½	cup quick-cooking barley

- Trim fat from meat; cut meat into ½-inch cubes. Combine beef cubes, water, celery, mushrooms, carrots, onion, salt, rosemary, pepper, and garlic in a Dutch oven. Bring to boiling; reduce heat. Cover and simmer 1 to 1¼ hours or until beef is tender. If necessary, skim the fat.

- Stir in tomato paste and quick-cooking barley. Return to boiling; reduce heat. Cover and simmer about 10 minutes or until barley is tender. Makes 8 servings.

Pork Tenderloin with Mushrooms

Per serving:
209 cal. (24% from fat), 29 g pro., 12 g carbo., 6 g fat,
81 mg cholesterol, 2 g dietary fiber, 320 mg sodium.

Preparation time:
15 minutes

Cooking time:
15 minutes

In addition to the low-calorie mushrooms and green onions, the lean pork tenderloin, low-fat yogurt, and skim milk all help to make this easy main dish light and lean.

6 ounces whole pork tenderloin

Nonstick spray coating

½ cup sliced fresh mushrooms

2 tablespoons sliced green onion

1 clove garlic, minced

¼ cup plain low-fat yogurt

3 tablespoons skim milk

2 teaspoons all-purpose flour

½ teaspoon instant chicken bouillon granules

Dash ground nutmeg

Dash pepper

• Trim fat from pork. Cut pork crosswise into 4 slices. Place each slice between two sheets of waxed paper. Using the flat side of a meat mallet, pound lightly to ¼-inch thickness.

• Spray a cold medium skillet with nonstick coating. Preheat skillet. Add pork and cook over medium heat about 3 minutes or until browned. Turn and cook 2 to 4 minutes more or until pork no longer is pink. Remove from skillet; cover and keep warm.

• Add mushrooms, green onion, and garlic to skillet. Cook and stir over medium heat until the vegetables are tender.

• Stir together yogurt, milk, flour, bouillon granules, nutmeg, and pepper. (Mixture may look curdled.) Add to mushroom mixture in skillet. Cook and stir until thickened and bubbly. Spoon sauce over meat served on two dinner plates. Makes 2 servings.

Margarine Update

Supermarket dairy cases host a variety of margarine and margarinelike products. Use the following descriptions to help you choose the products that are just what you need.

Regular margarines are available in salted and unsalted stick and block forms. They must be 80 percent fat and most often are made with a single vegetable oil. Using unsalted margarine and adding just a small amount of salt for flavor is one way to reduce sodium in recipes.

Diet margarines have 50 percent less fat than regular margarines, and contain more water. They usually are sold in tub form.

Vegetable-oil spreads contain more fat than diet margarine, but less fat than regular margarine. These products are available in both tub and stick forms, and sometimes are labeled "lite."

In general, diet margarine and vegetable-oil spreads contain added water, and are not recommended for cooking and baking unless the recipe specifies one of these products.

Skillet Pork Chops and Rice

Per serving:
310 cal. (15% from fat), 24 g pro., 41 g carbo., 5 g fat,
47 mg cholesterol, 3 g dietary fiber, 1,104 mg sodium.

Preparation time:
12 minutes

Cooking time:
25 minutes

This delicious meal-in-a-skillet works best if you use a firm cooking apple. Try Jonathan or Granny Smith apples. They'll cook up juicy and tender but still will hold their shape.

1½ cups water

½ cup chopped onion

¼ cup chopped green pepper

½ teaspoon ground cinnamon

⅔ cup long-grain rice

2 small cooking apples

12 ounces fully cooked boneless smoked pork chops

2 tablespoons lower-calorie orange marmalade

- Combine water, onion, green pepper, and cinnamon in a large skillet. Stir in *uncooked* rice. Bring to boiling; reduce heat. Cover and simmer for 15 minutes.

- Core apples and cut into thin wedges. Stir apples into rice mixture in skillet.

- Place chops on top of rice mixture. Cover and simmer 10 to 15 minutes more or until rice is tender and chops are heated through. Spread marmalade evenly over chops.

- Place pork chops on 4 dinner plates and spoon a mound of rice mixture beside each chop. Makes 4 servings.

Indonesian Pork Skewers

Per serving:
422 cal. (27% from fat), 26 g pro., 50 g carbo., 13 g fat,
77 mg cholesterol, 2 g dietary fiber, 200 mg sodium.

Preparation time:
20 minutes

Broiling time:
15 minutes

When threading these kabobs, leave a little space between the pieces so the heat reaches all sides and cooks the food more evenly. Be careful not to overcook the pork or it will become tough and lose some flavor.

¼ cup vinegar

¼ cup prepared mustard

¼ cup light molasses

2 tablespoons ginger preserves or orange marmalade

¼ teaspoon ground ginger

1½ pounds lean boneless pork, cut into 1-inch cubes

½ of a medium pineapple, halved lengthwise, cored, and cut into ½-inch-thick slices

1 red sweet pepper, cut into 1-inch pieces

3 cups hot cooked rice

- For sauce, combine vinegar, mustard, molasses, preserves, and ginger in a small bowl.

- Alternately thread pork cubes, pineapple slices, and pepper pieces on 12 skewers, leaving about ¼ inch between pieces.

- Place kabobs on the unheated rack of a broiler pan. Broil 4 to 5 inches from the heat for 10 minutes. Brush with sauce. Broil kabobs 5 to 8 minutes more or until pork no longer is pink, brushing with sauce occasionally. Heat remaining sauce in a small saucepan; pass with kabobs. Serve with hot cooked rice. If desired, garnish with green onion fans. Makes 6 servings.

Grilling Directions: Grill kabobs on an uncovered grill directly over *medium-hot* coals about 12 minutes or until pork no longer is pink, turning and brushing with sauce after 6 minutes.

Note: Pictured on pages 20–21.

Scalloped Potatoes and Ham

Per serving:
352 cal. (21% from fat), 21 g pro., 50 g carbo., 8 g fat,
33 mg cholesterol, 3 g dietary fiber, 852 mg sodium.

Preparation time:
20 minutes

Baking time:
1¼ hours

Standing time:
10 minutes

All hams are not created equal. Scout out the leanest lower-sodium ham available at your supermarket. That way you can keep the fat and sodium in this hunger-satisfying casserole to a minimum.

1   10¾-ounce can lower-sodium condensed cream of mushroom soup

½   cup skim milk

½   teaspoon dried marjoram, crushed

⅛   to ¼ teaspoon pepper

1½ cups cubed fully cooked lower-sodium ham (8 ounces)

1   cup chopped onion

4½ cups thinly sliced peeled potatoes (4 to 5 medium)

2   tablespoons fine dry bread crumbs

1   tablespoon snipped parsley

1   teaspoon margarine, melted

- For sauce, stir together the soup, milk, marjoram, and pepper in a bowl. Set aside.

- Layer *half* of each of the ham, onion, potatoes, and sauce in a 2-quart casserole. Repeat layers.

- Bake, covered, in a 350° oven about 1 hour or until potatoes are nearly tender. Stir together bread crumbs, parsley, and melted margarine in a small bowl. Sprinkle over casserole. Bake, uncovered, 15 minutes more or until potatoes are tender.

- Let stand for 10 minutes before serving. Serves 4.

Lentil-Ham Soup

Per serving:
215 cal. (11% from fat), 22 g pro., 27 g carbo., 3 g fat,
25 mg cholesterol, 6 g dietary fiber, 540 mg sodium.

Preparation time:
18 minutes

Cooking time:
33 minutes

To cut down on dishwashing, cut up the tomatoes right in the can. Just use a pair of kitchen shears to snip the tomatoes into bite-size pieces.

1   cup dry lentils

4   cups water

2   cups cubed fully cooked lower-sodium ham (10 ounces)

3   medium carrots, coarsely chopped

1   medium onion, chopped (½ cup)

1   bay leaf

¼   teaspoon pepper

¼   teaspoon dried marjoram, crushed

⅛   teaspoon garlic powder

1   16-ounce can tomatoes, cut up

3   tablespoons snipped parsley

- Rinse lentils. Combine lentils and water in a 4-quart Dutch oven.

- Stir cubed ham, the carrots, onion, bay leaf, pepper, marjoram, and garlic powder into lentils in the Dutch oven. Bring to boiling; reduce heat. Simmer, covered, about 30 minutes or until lentils are tender.

- Stir in *undrained* tomatoes and parsley. Heat through. Discard bay leaf. Makes 6 servings.

Chicken Parmigiano

Per serving:
177 cal. (22% from fat), 20 g pro., 14 g carbo., 4 g fat,
48 mg cholesterol, 0 g dietary fiber, 499 mg sodium.

**Preparation time:
10 minutes**

**Cooking time:
14 minutes**

This recipe is a slimmed-down version of Veal Parmigiano. Because the recipe uses chicken instead of veal, it has less than half the cholesterol. And because it calls for nonstick coating instead of cooking oil and skips the traditional mozzarella cheese, it also has less than a quarter of the fat of the classic.

¼ cup fine dry bread crumbs

2 tablespoons grated Parmesan cheese

4 skinless, boneless medium chicken breast halves

2 tablespoons skim milk

Nonstick spray coating

1 14 ½-ounce can stewed tomatoes

2 teaspoons cornstarch

½ teaspoon dried Italian seasoning, crushed

1 tablespoon grated Parmesan cheese

- Combine bread crumbs and the 2 tablespoons Parmesan cheese in a pie plate or on a sheet of waxed paper.

- Rinse chicken; pat dry. Brush chicken with milk. Coat with the crumb mixture. Spray a cold large skillet with nonstick spray coating. Preheat skillet, then add chicken. Cook over medium heat for 8 to 10 minutes or until tender and no longer pink, turning the pieces occasionally to brown evenly. Transfer to a platter; cover to keep warm. Wipe the skillet with paper towels.

- Combine stewed tomatoes, cornstarch, and Italian seasoning in the same skillet. Cook and stir until thickened and bubbly. Cook and stir 2 minutes more.

- Spoon tomato mixture over chicken. Sprinkle with the 1 tablespoon Parmesan cheese. Makes 4 servings.

Lean Ways with Chicken

You can make already-lean chicken even leaner by not eating its skin. There are two ways to do this. If the chicken will cook in a broth mixture, which will collect the fat from the skin, remove the skin before cooking. If you're baking or broiling the chicken, the fat will drain away from the meat, so you can wait until after cooking to remove the skin. Leaving the skin on the chicken while it bakes or broils keeps it moist and adds flavor, and removing the skin before eating the chicken will save you the extra calories and fat.

Poaching also is a healthy way to cook chicken (especially for recipes calling for cubed cooked chicken) because it doesn't require any added fat—the chicken simply simmers in water. For about 2½ cups of cooked cubed chicken, begin with 1 pound of skinless, boneless chicken breasts. Place the chicken in a saucepan with 1⅓ cups water. Bring to boiling; reduce heat and simmer 12 to 14 minutes or until the chicken is tender and no longer pink. [To poach in the microwave oven, place the chicken in a 1½-quart microwave-safe casserole. Micro-cook on 100% power (high) for 3 minutes. Turn over and rearrange the pieces. Cook, covered, on high 3 to 4 minutes more or until done.] Remove the chicken from the liquid and let it cool slightly. Then cut it into cubes. Cover and refrigerate the chicken for up to two days, or freeze it for up to three months.

Chicken-and-Apple Salad

Chicken-and-Apple Salad

Per serving:
260 cal. (28% from fat), 22 g pro., 27 g carbo., 9 g fat,
54 mg cholesterol, 3 g dietary fiber, 135 mg sodium.

**Preparation time:
15 minutes**

**Cooking time:
6 minutes**

If you can afford a little extra fat, sprinkle toasted chopped pecans over this main-dish salad. To toast the nuts, place them in a shallow baking dish and bake in a 350° oven for 5 to 10 minutes, stirring often.

2   tablespoons water

4   teaspoons olive oil or cooking oil

4   teaspoons honey

2   teaspoons Dijon-style mustard

2   teaspoons lemon juice

12 ounces skinless, boneless chicken breasts, cut into thin, bite-size strips

2   cups sliced fresh mushrooms

2   large red apples, cored and sliced

6   cups torn mixed greens

¼   cup toasted chopped pecans (optional)

• Combine water, oil, honey, mustard, and lemon juice in a large skillet. Bring to boiling. Add the chicken. Cook and stir over medium heat for 4 to 6 minutes or until chicken is tender and no longer pink. Remove chicken from skillet; cover and keep warm.

• Add sliced mushrooms and sliced apples to skillet. Cook, covered, for 2 to 3 minutes or until just tender. Stir in cooked chicken; heat through.

• Arrange greens on 4 serving plates; spoon chicken mixture on top. If desired, sprinkle with toasted chopped pecans. Makes 4 servings.

Honey-Mustard Chicken

Per serving:
174 cal. (18% from fat), 25 g pro., 9 g carbo., 3 g fat,
69 mg cholesterol, 0 g dietary fiber, 149 mg sodium.

**Preparation time:
8 minutes**

**Broiling time:
30 minutes**

When time is at a premium, turn to this great-tasting recipe for a dinner on the double. The simple glaze goes together in just a minute or two while the chicken is broiling.

2   whole medium chicken breasts (about 1½ pounds), skinned and halved lengthwise

2   tablespoons honey

1   tablespoon Dijon-style mustard

1   tablespoon lemon juice

½   teaspoon poppy seeds

¼   teaspoon pepper

• Rinse chicken; pat dry. Place chicken, bone side up, on the unheated rack of a broiler pan. Broil chicken 4 to 5 inches from the heat for 15 minutes. Turn. Continue broiling for 10 minutes.

• Meanwhile, combine honey, Dijon-style mustard, lemon juice, poppy seeds, and pepper in a small bowl. Stir together well.

• Brush chicken with honey-mustard mixture. Broil about 5 minutes more or until chicken is tender and no longer pink. Makes 4 servings.

Chicken Gazpacho

Chicken Gazpacho

Per serving:
247 cal. (14% from fat), 25 g pro., 28 g carbo., 4 g fat, 54 mg cholesterol, 2 g dietary fiber, 1,030 mg sodium.

Preparation time:
15 minutes

Cooking time:
3½ minutes

Baking time:
10 minutes

Chilling time:
4 hours

Gazpacho is a traditional Spanish side-dish soup that's served chilled. This adaptation of the old favorite includes chicken so it's hearty enough to be a main dish.

Nonstick spray coating

12   ounces skinless, boneless chicken breasts

½   teaspoon ground cumin

1   14½-ounce can Mexican-style stewed tomatoes

1   medium cucumber or zucchini, chopped

1   small green pepper, coarsely chopped

¼   cup sliced celery

¼   cup sliced green onions

1   tablespoon vinegar

2   teaspoons chicken bouillon granules

½   teaspoon dried basil, crushed

Dash bottled hot pepper sauce

Toasted Pita Strips (see recipe, above right)

- Spray a cold large skillet with nonstick coating. Rinse chicken; pat dry. Cut chicken into ½-inch pieces.

- Preheat skillet over medium heat. Add chicken to skillet. Stir-fry 3 to 4 minutes or until tender and no longer pink. Sprinkle chicken with cumin; stir-fry 30 seconds more.

- Transfer chicken to a large bowl. Cut up any large tomatoes; add tomatoes, cucumber, green pepper, celery, green onions, vinegar, bouillon granules, basil, and hot pepper sauce to chicken in bowl. Stir in 1 cup *water*. Cover and chill 4 to 24 hours. Serve with Toasted Pita Strips. If desired, garnish soup with fresh cilantro or parsley. Makes 4 servings.

Toasted Pita Strips: Cut 2 *pita bread rounds* in half crosswise. Split each half apart. Cut the pieces into 1-inch strips. Spread in a single layer on a baking sheet. Bake in a 350° oven about 10 minutes or until crisp. Cool on a wire rack.

Easy Oven-Fried Chicken

Per serving:
150 cal. (23% from fat), 24 g pro., 3 g carbo., 4 g fat, 65 mg cholesterol, 0 g dietary fiber, 107 mg sodium.

Preparation time:
15 minutes

Baking time:
45 minutes

If you love fried chicken but have given it up because it's too high in fat, try this lip-smacking recipe. Using chicken breasts without the skin and oven-frying the breasts helps eliminate much of the fat of traditional fried chicken.

3   medium chicken breasts, skinned

¼   cup cornflake crumbs

1   tablespoon snipped fresh parsley

⅓   cup plain low-fat yogurt

1   clove garlic, minced

2   teaspoons Worcestershire sauce or white wine Worcestershire sauce

Dash ground red pepper

- Halve chicken breasts lengthwise. Rinse chicken; pat dry. Place on a rack in a shallow baking pan; set aside.

- Combine cornflake crumbs and parsley in a small mixing bowl; set aside.

- Combine yogurt, garlic, Worcestershire sauce, and red pepper in another small mixing bowl.

- Brush chicken with yogurt mixture, then sprinkle with crumb mixture.

- Bake, uncovered, in a 375° oven for 45 to 55 minutes or until chicken is tender and no longer pink. Serves 6.

Chicken Tacos

Cashew-Chicken Stir-Fry

Per serving:
343 cal. (27% from fat), 21 g pro., 41 g carbo., 10 g fat,
41 mg cholesterol, 4 g dietary fiber, 730 mg sodium.

Preparation time:
15 minutes

Cooking time:
12 minutes

Fresh gingerroot adds a pleasant spiciness to this flavorful dish. If you can't find gingerroot in the produce section of your supermarket, use ½ teaspoon ground ginger instead.

1	6-ounce package frozen pea pods, thawed
⅔	cup cold water
2	tablespoons soy sauce
2	teaspoons cornstarch
½	teaspoon instant chicken bouillon granules
	Nonstick spray coating
2	cloves garlic, minced
1	to 2 teaspoons grated gingerroot
2	carrots, thinly sliced
3	green onions, sliced
1	tablespoon cooking oil
3	skinless, boneless chicken breast halves, cut into bite-size strips (about 9 ounces)
2	cups hot cooked rice
¼	cup cashews

- Cut pea pods in half. Combine water, soy sauce, cornstarch, and bouillon granules in a bowl.

- Spray a cold wok or large skillet with nonstick coating. Preheat over medium-high heat. Add garlic and gingerroot; stir-fry 30 seconds. Add carrots; stir-fry 2 minutes. Add green onions; stir-fry 1 minute or until carrots are crisp-tender. Remove vegetables from wok.

- Add oil to the wok. Add chicken; stir-fry 2 to 3 minutes or until chicken is tender and no longer pink. Push chicken from center of wok.

- Stir cornstarch mixture; add to the center of the wok. Cook and stir until thickened and bubbly. Return vegetables to the wok. Stir in pea pods. Cook and stir 2 minutes more. Serve with rice; sprinkle with nuts. Makes 4 servings.

Chicken Tacos

Per serving:
311 cal. (21% from fat), 22 g pro., 39 g carbo., 7 g fat,
43 mg cholesterol, 4 g dietary fiber, 779 mg sodium.

Preparation time:
15 minutes

Cooking time:
8 minutes

This family favorite keeps the fat in line by using chicken instead of ground beef. No cooked chicken on hand? Check out the tip on page 31 for cooking hints.

	Nonstick spray coating
1	cup chopped onion
1	clove garlic, minced
2	cups chopped cooked chicken breast
1	8-ounce can tomato sauce
1	4-ounce can chopped green chili peppers, drained
12	6- or 7-inch flour tortillas
2	medium tomatoes
2	cups shredded lettuce
¾	cup finely shredded, lower-fat mild cheddar cheese (3 ounces)

- Spray a cold 10-inch skillet with nonstick spray coating. Add onion and garlic; cook until tender. Stir in chicken, tomato sauce, and green chili peppers. Cook and stir until heated through.

- Meanwhile, wrap tortillas in foil. Heat in a 300° oven about 10 minutes to soften.

- Seed and chop tomatoes. Divide chicken mixture among flour tortillas. Top with lettuce, tomato, and cheese. Makes 6 servings.

Turkey Kabobs

Per serving:
157 cal. (4% from fat), 21 g pro., 17 g carbo., 1 g fat,
55 mg cholesterol, 1 g dietary fiber, 575 mg sodium.

Preparation time:
15 minutes

Marinating time:
30 minutes

Cooking time:
8 minutes

Red pepper and gingerroot give a pleasant zing to the turkey and vegetables. To make the marinating step easy, marinate the turkey in a Tupperware® 6-cup Wonderlier® bowl.

⅓ cup red wine vinegar

3 tablespoons corn syrup

2 tablespoons soy sauce

1½ teaspoons grated gingerroot

¼ teaspoon garlic powder

¼ teaspoon crushed red pepper

12 ounces turkey breast tenderloin steaks

1 small zucchini

1 small yellow crookneck squash

1 medium red sweet pepper

- For marinade, combine vinegar, corn syrup, soy sauce, gingerroot, garlic powder, and crushed red pepper in a medium bowl.

- Rinse turkey; pat dry. Cut lengthwise into ½-inch-wide strips. Add to marinade; stir to coat. Let turkey stand at room temperature for 30 minutes or chill for 1 hour, stirring occasionally.

- Cut zucchini and yellow squash into ¾-inch slices. Cut any large pieces in half. Cut red sweet pepper into 1-inch squares.

- Remove turkey from marinade, reserving marinade. On four 10- or 12-inch skewers, thread turkey strips, accordion-style, around zucchini, yellow squash, and pepper pieces. (See tip below.)

- Place on the unheated rack of a broiler pan. Broil 3 to 4 inches from the heat for 5 minutes. Brush turkey and vegetables with marinade; turn kabobs. Broil 3 to 5 minutes more or until turkey is no longer pink and vegetables are tender. Makes 4 servings.

Note: To grill kabobs, cook on an uncovered grill over *medium-hot* coals for 10 to 12 minutes or until turkey no longer is pink and vegetables are tender, turning once and brushing with marinade during the last 5 minutes.

Kabob Know-How

For attractive-looking and evenly cooked Turkey Kabobs every time, follow these easy directions. First, remove the turkey strips from the marinade and drain them on paper towels. Then, using 10- to 12-inch skewers, thread one end of a turkey strip onto the skewer, staying close to the point of the skewer. Next, add a slice of zucchini and fold the turkey strip over the zucchini, securing it onto the skewer. Now, add a slice of yellow squash and fold the turkey strip over the squash, securing it onto the skewer. Finally, add a red pepper square and fold the rest of the turkey strip over the pepper square, securing it onto the skewer.

Carefully slide all of the pieces down the skewer, being sure to allow a little space between them so the heat will circulate around them. Repeat the threading process until the skewer is full. Fill the rest of the skewers in the same way.

Turkey-Vegetable Fajitas

Per serving:
373 cal. (20% from fat), 26 g pro., 48 g carbo., 8 g fat,
55 mg cholesterol, 3 g dietary fiber, 818 mg sodium.

Preparation time:
15 minutes

Cooking time:
10 minutes

Bring this zesty vegetable-and-turkey combo to the table in a pretty skillet—just the way restaurants do. Then everyone can fill and roll up a tortilla.

4   10-inch flour tortillas

¼   cup sodium-reduced soy sauce

2   tablespoons sugar

2   tablespoons lemon juice

1   tablespoon cornstarch

¼   teaspoon crushed red pepper

    Nonstick spray coating

3   green, red, or yellow sweet peppers, cut into strips

1   medium onion, chopped

3   cloves garlic, minced

1   tablespoon olive oil

12 ounces turkey breast tenderloin steaks, cut into thin strips

- Wrap tortillas in foil; warm in a 300° oven about 10 minutes. Combine soy sauce, sugar, lemon juice, cornstarch, and crushed red pepper in a bowl.

- Spray a cold large skillet with nonstick coating; preheat. Add sweet peppers, onion, and garlic. Stir-fry 3 to 4 minutes. Remove vegetables from skillet.

- Add oil to the skillet. Stir-fry turkey for 3 to 4 minutes or until no longer pink.

- Stir soy sauce mixture; add to the skillet. Cook and stir until bubbly. Add vegetables; heat through. Spoon turkey mixture onto tortillas; roll up. Makes 4 servings.

Italian-Style Turkey Steaks

Per serving:
278 cal. (17% from fat), 28 g pro., 30 g carbo., 5 g fat,
60 mg cholesterol, 4 g dietary fiber, 423 mg sodium.

Preparation time:
5 minutes

Cooking time:
12 minutes

Sometimes, turkey cuts can be confusing. For this recipe, purchase crosswise cuts from the turkey breast that are ½ to 1 inch thick.

4   ounces green noodles or fettuccine

6   cups hot water

2   teaspoons cooking oil

4   boneless turkey breast steaks (about 12 ounces total)

2   cups whole fresh mushrooms

1   14½-ounce can stewed tomatoes

1   teaspoon dried minced onion

½   teaspoon dried oregano, crushed

¼   cup grated Parmesan cheese

- Cook pasta according to package directions, *except* use a large saucepan and the hot water.

- Meanwhile, heat oil until hot in a large nonstick skillet. Cook boneless turkey steaks in hot oil about 2 minutes on each side or until browned. Meanwhile, cut mushrooms into quarters.

- Remove turkey steaks from skillet, reserving drippings in skillet. Cook mushrooms in drippings for 3 minutes. Remove skillet from heat and add *undrained* tomatoes, onion, and oregano. Return turkey to the skillet. Return to heat and bring to boiling. Boil rapidly, uncovered, about 2 minutes or until liquid is slightly reduced and turkey is tender and no longer pink.

- Transfer turkey and sauce to a serving plate. Sprinkle Parmesan cheese over turkey steaks. Drain pasta. Serve turkey and sauce with pasta. Makes 4 servings.

Fish Bundles with Rice

Turkey Waldorf Salad

Per serving:
191 cal. (20% from fat), 23 g pro., 17 g carbo., 4 g fat,
55 mg cholesterol, 2 g dietary fiber, 223 mg sodium.

Preparation time:
12 minutes

Chilling time:
1 hour

This colorful, creamy salad is a main-dish variation of the American side-dish favorite. Leave the peel on the apples for extra color and more fiber.

2 cups cubed cooked turkey or chicken

4 small apples, chopped (2 cups)

1 cup chopped celery

4 green onions, sliced

½ cup plain low-fat yogurt

¼ cup nonfat or lower-calorie mayonnaise or salad dressing

4 teaspoons lemon juice

1 teaspoon sugar

- Combine turkey, apple, celery, and green onions in a medium mixing bowl. Stir together yogurt, mayonnaise or salad dressing, lemon juice, and sugar in another small bowl.

- Pour yogurt mixture over turkey mixture. Toss to mix well. Cover and chill for 1 to 3 hours. Makes 4 servings.

Fish Bundles with Rice

Per serving:
256 cal. (6% from fat), 25 g pro., 34 g carbo., 2 g fat,
51 mg cholesterol, 3 g dietary fiber, 430 mg sodium.

Preparation time:
18 minutes

Cooking time:
30 minutes

Impress dinner guests with these elegant fish rolls. For a show-stopping presentation, arrange the rolls on grape leaves, and garnish with lemon wedges and clusters of grapes.

4 4-ounce fresh or frozen sole or flounder fillets

½ teaspoon lemon-pepper seasoning

1 small zucchini

1 small yellow summer squash

4 green onions

Paprika

1⅓ cups water

1 teaspoon instant chicken bouillon granules

1½ cups quick-cooking rice

2 cups lightly packed fresh spinach, snipped

- Thaw fish fillets, if frozen. Sprinkle fillets with lemon-pepper seasoning.

- Cut zucchini and yellow squash into thin matchstick pieces about 2½ inches long. Cut green onions into slivers about 2½ inches long. Gather vegetables into 4 bundles and place crosswise on centers of fish fillets. Roll fish fillets around vegetable bundles.

- Place fish rolls, seam side down, in a 2-quart square baking dish. Sprinkle fish rolls with paprika. Bake, covered, in a 350° oven for 25 minutes. Uncover and bake 5 to 10 minutes more or until fish just flakes when tested with a fork.

- Meanwhile, combine water and chicken bouillon granules in a saucepan. Bring to boiling. Remove from heat. Stir in rice and spinach; cover and let stand 5 minutes. Fluff with a fork before serving.

- Transfer fish to serving plates. Serve rice with fish. Makes 4 servings.

Grilled Halibut with Cucumber Sauce

Per serving:
204 cal. (20% from fat), 36 g pro., 5 g carbo., 4 g fat,
53 mg cholesterol, 0 g dietary fiber, 233 mg sodium.

Preparation time:
10 minutes

Grilling time:
8 minutes

This tantalizing yet simple-to-make recipe is ideal for a special dinner for two. For small, attractively shaped halibut steaks, select those that have been cut from the tail end of the fish.

2   fresh or frozen halibut steaks, cut ¾ inch thick (6 ounces each)

¼   cup finely chopped seeded cucumber

3   tablespoons plain nonfat yogurt

1   tablespoon nonfat mayonnaise or salad dressing

1   teaspoon snipped chives

   Dash salt

   Dash pepper

   Nonstick spray coating

1   tablespoon lemon juice

● Thaw fish, if frozen. For sauce, stir together cucumber, yogurt, mayonnaise or salad dressing, chives, salt, and pepper in a small bowl. Cover and chill in the refrigerator until needed.

● To grill, spray a cold grill rack with nonstick coating. Place fish on the rack. Brush fish with some of the lemon juice. Grill fish on an uncovered grill directly over *medium-hot* coals for 4 minutes. Using a wide spatula, carefully turn the fish over. Brush with the remaining lemon juice and grill 4 to 7 minutes more or until fish just flakes when tested with a fork.

● Serve fish with the cucumber sauce. If desired, garnish with lemon peel strips and chives. Makes 2 servings.

Note: To broil the fish steaks, spray the unheated rack of a broiler pan with nonstick coating. Place fish steaks on the rack. Brush fish steaks with some of the lemon juice. Broil 4 inches from the heat for 4 minutes. Turn fish over and brush with the remaining lemon juice. Broil 4 to 7 minutes more or until fish just flakes when tested with a fork.

Dressing Up Broiled Fish

When you're looking for a healthy, fast meal, nothing beats broiled fish. You can have it on the table in minutes. But plain fish can get boring. Here are some easy low-fat ways to add unique flavor and variety to this healthy main dish.

Stir together plain lower-fat yogurt, shredded zucchini, and a little dillweed to spoon on top of the cooked fish.

Use your favorite lower-fat salad dressing as a marinade or dipping sauce for the fish.

Squeeze fresh lemon juice over the fish and sprinkle it with fresh snipped chives or parsley.

Mix equal parts of lower-fat mayonnaise or salad dressing and plain lower-fat yogurt with a little curry powder and spoon it over the cooked fish.

Sprinkle a mixture of Italian-seasoned bread crumbs and finely shredded or grated Parmesan cheese on the fish during the last few minutes of broiling.

Flounder Dijon

Per serving:
101 cal. (13% from fat), 16 g pro., 5 g carbo., 1 g fat,
41 mg cholesterol, 1 g dietary fiber, 331 mg sodium.

Preparation time:
10 minutes

Baking time:
4 minutes

Cooking time:
12 minutes

Flounder is a mild-flavored fish with a fine texture. It is sold under various names such as winter or summer flounder, sanddab flounder, gray sole, and fluke.

4	3-ounce fresh or frozen flounder fillets
	Nonstick spray coating
½	cup sliced fresh mushrooms
⅓	cup sliced zucchini
¼	cup thin carrot strips cut 1 inch long
¼	cup sliced green onions
¾	cup skim milk
1½	teaspoons cornstarch
1½	teaspoons Dijon-style mustard
1	teaspoon instant chicken bouillon granules

- Thaw fish, if frozen. Measure thickness of fish. Place fish in a single layer in a 2-quart rectangular baking dish; tuck under thin edges. Bake in a 450° oven until fish just flakes when tested with a fork. Allow 4 to 6 minutes for each ½-inch thickness of fish.

- Meanwhile, for sauce, spray a cold medium saucepan with nonstick coating. Preheat over medium heat.

- Cook sliced mushrooms, sliced zucchini, carrot strips, and green onions in the saucepan until vegetables are crisp-tender.

- Stir together skim milk, cornstarch, Dijon-style mustard, and chicken bouillon granules. Add milk mixture to vegetables in saucepan.

- Cook and stir until the mixture is thickened and bubbly. Cook and stir 2 minutes more.

- Transfer fish to dinner plates. Ladle the vegetable sauce over fish. If desired, serve with asparagus spears garnished with a twist of lemon. Makes 4 servings.

Crispy Baked Halibut

Per serving:
213 cal. (30% from fat), 32 g pro., 4 g carbo., 7 g fat,
48 mg cholesterol, 0 g dietary fiber, 178 mg sodium.

Preparation time:
12 minutes

Baking time:
8 minutes

To accent the flavor of the Parmesan-cheese coated halibut, just squirt a little juice from a lemon wedge onto the fish.

1¼	pounds fresh or frozen halibut steaks, cut 1 inch thick
2	teaspoons cooking oil
¾	cup soft bread crumbs
2	tablespoons grated Parmesan cheese
1	tablespoon snipped fresh tarragon or ½ teaspoon dried tarragon, crushed
½	teaspoon paprika
	Dash pepper
	Lemon wedges (optional)

- Thaw fish, if frozen. Cut fish into four portions; pat dry and brush with cooking oil. Stir together bread crumbs, Parmesan cheese, tarragon, paprika, and pepper in a shallow baking dish. Dip fish pieces into crumb mixture to coat both sides. Arrange pieces in a 2-quart rectangular baking dish. Sprinkle any leftover bread-crumb mixture on top.

- Bake fish, uncovered, in a 450° oven 8 to 12 minutes or until fish just flakes when tested with a fork. *Do not turn during baking.* If desired, serve with lemon wedges. Makes 4 servings.

Shrimp Fajitas

Sweet-and-Sour Fish

Per serving:
287 cal. (4% from fat), 22 g pro., 46 g carbo., 1 g fat,
45 mg cholesterol, 1 g dietary fiber, 704 mg sodium.

Preparation time:
10 minutes

Cooking time:
9 minutes

Just about any fish fillet will work for this recipe. Whatever kind of fish you choose, this delicious dish goes together in a hurry.

1   pound fresh or frozen cod or other fish fillets, cut ½ inch thick

½   teaspoon instant chicken bouillon granules

1   medium green or red sweet pepper, cut into 1-inch squares (1 cup)

1   carrot, thinly sliced

1   clove garlic, minced

2   tablespoons brown sugar

4   teaspoons cornstarch

2   tablespoons vinegar

2   tablespoons soy sauce

½   cup seedless grapes, halved

2   cups hot cooked rice

• Thaw fish, if frozen. Cut into ¾-inch pieces. Add 1 cup *water* to a large skillet. Bring to boiling. Carefully add fish pieces. Return just to boiling; reduce heat. Cover and simmer for 4 to 6 minutes or until fish just flakes when tested with a fork. Remove fish from skillet; discard liquid.

• Combine bouillon granules and ½ cup *water* in same skillet used to boil fish. Add green pepper squares, sliced carrot, and minced garlic. Bring to boiling; reduce heat. Cover and simmer for 4 minutes or until vegetables are nearly tender. *Do not drain.*

• Combine brown sugar, cornstarch, vinegar, and soy sauce. Stir into vegetable mixture. Cook and stir until thickened and bubbly. Cook and stir 1 minute more.

• Gently stir in fish and grapes. Heat through. Serve with hot cooked rice. Makes 4 servings.

Shrimp Fajitas

Per serving:
290 cal. (22% from fat), 20 g pro., 37 g carbo., 7 g fat,
125 mg cholesterol, 3 g dietary fiber, 605 mg sodium.

Preparation time:
12 minutes

Marinating time:
20 minutes

Cooking time:
5 minutes

A Tupperware® 26-ounce One Touch™ serving bowl is ideal for marinating the shrimp. They'll get a wonderfully tangy bite from the lemon-juice-and-chili-powder marinade.

12   ounces fresh or frozen shelled medium shrimp

2   teaspoons cooking oil

2   teaspoons lemon juice

½   teaspoon ground cumin

¼   teaspoon chili powder

1   clove garlic, minced

8   6- or 7-inch flour tortillas

     Nonstick spray coating

2   medium carrots, cut into matchstick pieces (1 cup)

4   green onions, cut into 1-inch pieces

8   small leaf-lettuce leaves

     Bottled salsa

• Thaw shrimp, if frozen. Combine oil, lemon juice, cumin, chili powder, and garlic in a bowl. Add shrimp. Stir to coat with marinade. Let stand at room temperature 20 minutes, stirring occasionally.

• Wrap tortillas in foil and warm in a 300° oven about 10 minutes.

• Spray a cold skillet with nonstick spray coating. Add carrots; cook over medium heat 2 minutes or until nearly tender. Add green onions to skillet; cook 1 minute. Add shrimp and marinade. Cook and stir over medium-high heat 2 to 3 minutes or until shrimp turn pink.

• Place a lettuce leaf atop each tortilla; spread with some salsa. Top with shrimp mixture. Fold edges over and secure with a wooden toothpick. Spoon additional salsa over each. Makes 4 servings.

Fish Creole

Per serving:
159 cal. (11% from fat), 25 g pro., 10 g carbo., 2 g fat,
42 mg cholesterol, 2 g dietary fiber, 406 mg sodium.

Preparation time:
10 minutes

Cooking time:
22 minutes

This healthy version of the New Orleans specialty, Shrimp Creole, uses fish instead of shrimp to help lower the cholesterol. It also cooks the onion, green pepper, and celery in water rather than the more traditional butter or cooking oil to cut fat.

1	pound fresh or frozen cod or other fish fillets
1	medium onion, chopped
½	cup chopped green pepper
½	cup chopped celery
¼	cup water
1	16-ounce can tomatoes, cut up
1	bay leaf
2	tablespoons snipped parsley
½	teaspoon garlic powder
¼	teaspoon salt
⅛	teaspoon ground red pepper
2	tablespoons cold water
1	tablespoon cornstarch

● Thaw fish, if frozen. Cut into 4 serving-size portions. Measure thickness of fish.

● Combine chopped onion, green pepper, celery, and the ¼ cup water in a large skillet. Bring to boiling; reduce heat. Simmer, covered, about 5 minutes or until vegetables are tender.

● Stir in *undrained* tomatoes, bay leaf, parsley, garlic powder, salt, and red pepper. Bring to boiling; reduce heat. Simmer, covered, for 5 minutes. Add fish. Allowing 4 to 6 minutes per ½-inch thickness of fish, cook until fish just flakes when tested with a fork. With a slotted spatula, transfer fish to a platter. Cover to keep warm.

● Stir together the 2 tablespoons water and the cornstarch. Stir into tomato mixture. Cook and stir until thickened and bubbly. Cook and stir 2 minutes more. Discard bay leaf. Serve sauce over fish. Makes 4 servings.

Dried-Bean Tactics

Although red meat, poultry, and fish are well-known sources of protein, less familiar ones include dried beans, dried peas, and lentils. These vegetables are especially appealing in a low-fat diet because they contain no cholesterol and almost no fat. In fact, you can maintain the protein in meat dishes and cut the fat and cholesterol by reducing the amount of meat you use and including cooked dried beans, peas, or lentils instead. This approach works well in main dishes such as soups, stews, meat sauces, and casseroles. You can choose from red kidney beans, pinto beans, navy or great northern beans, black-eyed peas, lima beans, red or black beans, garbanzo beans, lentils, and split peas.

Seafood Chowder

Per serving:
190 cal. (10% from fat), 29 g pro., 15 g carbo., 2 g fat,
117 mg cholesterol, 4 g dietary fiber, 1,244 mg sodium.

Preparation time:
20 minutes

Cooking time:
15 minutes

Warm and comforting on a cold winter day, this fish-and-vegetable combo can go together in minutes. Just use a microwave-safe dish, such as the Tupperware® 1-quart TupperWave® casserole, to thaw the fish and then the shrimp in the microwave oven.

12 ounces fresh or frozen cod or other fish fillets

8 ounces fresh or frozen peeled and deveined shrimp

2 cups chicken broth

1 cup sliced fresh mushrooms

1 large carrot, sliced

1 medium onion, chopped

1 clove garlic, minced

½ teaspoon dried marjoram, crushed

1 bay leaf

1 15-ounce can tomato sauce

2 large tomatoes, peeled, seeded, and chopped

2 tablespoons snipped parsley

½ teaspoon finely shredded lemon peel

- Thaw fish and shrimp, if frozen. Cut fish into 1-inch pieces. Set aside.

- Combine broth, mushrooms, carrot, onion, garlic, marjoram, bay leaf, ⅛ teaspoon *salt*, and ⅛ teaspoon *pepper* in a large saucepan. Bring to boiling; reduce heat. Cover and simmer for 10 minutes or until vegetables are tender.

- Stir in tomato sauce, tomatoes, fish, and shrimp. Return to boiling; reduce heat. Cover and simmer for 2 to 3 minutes or until fish just flakes when tested with a fork. Discard bay leaf. Sprinkle with parsley and lemon peel. Makes 4 servings.

Rice-and-Bean-Stuffed Peppers

Per serving:
234 cal. (6% from fat), 11 g pro., 46 g carbo., 2 g fat,
4 mg cholesterol, 9 g dietary fiber, 648 mg sodium.

Preparation time:
20 minutes

Baking time:
15 minutes

A tasty mixture of corn, rice, and kidney beans fills the sweet pepper shells in this low-fat meatless main dish. A sprinkle of mozzarella adds just a hint of cheese flavor.

2 large green, yellow, or red sweet peppers

1 cup frozen whole-kernel corn

½ cup chopped onion

1 8-ounce can tomato sauce with herbs

⅔ cup quick-cooking rice

2 tablespoons water

½ teaspoon sugar

1 16-ounce can red kidney beans, drained

¼ cup shredded mozz-arella cheese (1 ounce)

- Halve peppers lengthwise, removing stem ends, seeds, and membranes. Immerse peppers into *boiling water* for 3 minutes. Invert onto paper towels to drain well.

- Cook corn and onion in a small saucepan in a small amount of *boiling water* 5 minutes or until tender. Drain and return mixture to saucepan.

- Stir tomato sauce, *uncooked* rice, the 2 tablespoons water, the sugar, and ¼ teaspoon *pepper* into mixture in saucepan. Heat to boiling. Remove from heat; cover and let stand 5 minutes. Stir in beans.

- Place pepper halves, cut side up, in a 2-quart square baking dish. Mound rice mixture into pepper shells. Bake in a 375° oven 15 to 20 minutes or until heated through. Sprinkle with the cheese. Let stand 1 to 2 minutes or until cheese is melted. Makes 4 servings.

Vegetable-and-Cheese Sandwiches

Bean-and-Cheese Burritos

Per serving:
434 cal. (26% from fat), 23 g pro., 59 g carbo., 13 g fat,
25 mg cholesterol, 11 g dietary fiber, 1,502 mg sodium.

Preparation time:
15 minutes

Cooking time:
5 minutes

Baking time:
10 minutes

Cooking the onion in water instead of oil, substituting smaller tortillas, and using lower-fat cheese eliminates a lot of calories, fat, and cholesterol from this flavorful Tex-Mex dish.

8	6-inch flour tortillas
1	cup chopped onion (1 large)
2	tablespoons water
1	16-ounce can vegetarian refried beans
1	4-ounce can diced green chili peppers, drained
	Several dashes bottled hot pepper sauce
1¼	cups shredded lower-fat Monterey Jack cheese (5 ounces)
3	cups shredded lettuce
½	cup bottled salsa

- Wrap tortillas in foil. Heat in a 300° oven about 10 minutes to soften.

- Meanwhile, cook the onion in the water in a medium saucepan until tender. *Do not drain.* Stir in the refried beans, diced green chili peppers, and hot pepper sauce. Cook and stir until heated through.

- Spoon about *⅓ cup* of the bean mixture onto *each* tortilla just below the center. For each burrito, sprinkle about *3 tablespoons* of the cheese atop the bean mixture; roll up tortilla. Place on a foil-lined baking sheet.

- Bake, loosely covered, in a 350° oven about 10 minutes or until heated through. To serve, place ¾ cup of the shredded lettuce on each plate and top with 2 burritos. Serve with the salsa. Makes 4 servings.

Vegetable-and-Cheese Sandwiches

Per serving:
207 cal. (18% from fat), 18 g pro., 26 g carbo., 4 g fat,
8 mg cholesterol, 6 g dietary fiber, 704 mg sodium.

Preparation time:
15 minutes

If someone in your family takes a lunch to school or work, pack the fixings for these sandwiches in Tupperware® brand containers. First, spread the bread with the horseradish mustard, top with the spinach leaves, and put in a container. Then, put the cottage cheese mixture in another container. Finally, pack the containers and a frozen ice pack in a lunch bag. At lunchtime, assembling the sandwich is easy.

1½	cups low-fat cottage cheese, drained
¼	cup shredded carrot
¼	cup chopped green pepper or celery
½	teaspoon finely snipped chives
¼	cup plain low-fat yogurt
8	small slices whole wheat or white French bread
2	tablespoons horseradish mustard
	Spinach leaves
4	slices tomato, halved

- Stir together drained cottage cheese, shredded carrot, chopped green pepper or celery, and finely snipped chives in a small mixing bowl. Stir in plain yogurt.

- Spread the whole wheat or white French bread slices with horseradish mustard; top with spinach leaves. Spoon cottage cheese mixture onto bread slices. Top with tomato slices. Garnish with parsley, if desired. Makes 4 servings.

Vegetable Lasagna Rolls

Per serving:
319 cal. (29% from fat), 17 g pro., 40 g carbo., 11g fat,
25 mg cholesterol, 2 g dietary fiber, 530 mg sodium.

Preparation time:
30 minutes

Baking time:
35 minutes

Standing time:
10 minutes

For easy entertaining, make these flavor-packed lasagna rolls and chill them. Then pop the casserole in the oven and you'll be free to join your guests for appetizers while it bakes. Just remember to add about 15 minutes extra baking time because the rolls go in the oven chilled.

6	lasagna noodles
1	10-ounce package frozen chopped spinach
1	cup part-skim ricotta cheese
½	teaspoon dried basil, crushed
¼	teaspoon dried oregano, crushed
¼	teaspoon pepper
2	cups sliced fresh mushrooms
½	cup chopped onion
¼	cup water
1½	cups spaghetti sauce
1	cup shredded part-skim mozzarella cheese (4 ounces)
2	tablespoons finely shredded Parmesan cheese

- Cook noodles according to the package directions, *except* omit salt. Drain. Rinse with cold water and drain again. Cook spinach according to the package directions, *except* omit salt. Drain well.

- Stir together ricotta cheese, basil, oregano, and pepper in a small mixing bowl.

- Combine mushrooms, onion, and water in a small saucepan. Bring to boiling. Cover and cook about 5 minutes or until vegetables are tender. Drain well. Stir in spaghetti sauce. Cook and stir until heated through.

- To assemble rolls, cut cooked lasagna noodles in half crosswise. Spread *half* of the sauce mixture over the noodles. Top with *all* of the spinach, *all* of the ricotta-cheese mixture, and *all* of the mozzarella cheese. Loosely roll up the noodles and place in a greased 2-quart rectangular baking dish.

- Spoon the remaining sauce mixture over the rolls. Cover the dish with foil and bake in a 350° oven for 30 minutes. Uncover and bake 5 to 10 minutes more or until heated through. Sprinkle with Parmesan cheese. Let stand for 10 minutes before serving. Garnish with fresh basil, if desired. Serves 6.

Note: Pictured on the cover.

Layered Vegetable Lasagna

If you'd rather have traditional layered lasagna instead of lasagna rolls, follow these simple steps. First arrange *half* of the cooked lasagna noodles in a 2-quart rectangular baking dish. Cut the noodles to fit, if necessary. Top the noodles with *half* of the sauce mixture, *all* of the spinach, *all* of the ricotta-cheese mixture, and *half* of the mozzarella cheese. Then finish the casserole by layering on the remaining lasagna noodles, mozzarella cheese, and sauce mixture. Cover the dish with foil and bake in a 350° oven for 30 minutes. Uncover and bake 5 to 10 minutes more or until the lasagna is heated through. Sprinkle with Parmesan cheese. Let the lasagna stand for 10 minutes before cutting it.

Meatless Chili Soup

Per serving:
301 cal. (10% from fat), 18 g pro., 57 g carbo., 4 g fat,
1 mg cholesterol, 12 g dietary fiber, 956 mg sodium.

Preparation time:
12 minutes

Cooking time:
20 minutes

Serve bowls of this steaming soup with crisp bread sticks. Round out the meal with crispy carrots and celery to dunk in your favorite lower-fat dip or salad dressing.

1 15-ounce can garbanzo beans

1 15-ounce can red kidney beans

1 14½-ounce can beef broth

1 11-ounce can whole-kernel corn with sweet peppers, drained

1 10-ounce can tomatoes with green chili peppers

1 medium onion, chopped

2 teaspoons chili powder

⅛ teaspoon garlic powder

¼ teaspoon crushed red pepper

¼ cup plain low-fat yogurt

- Rinse and drain canned beans. Stir together garbanzo beans, kidney beans, beef broth, corn with sweet peppers, *undrained* tomatoes with green chili peppers, onion, chili power, garlic powder, red pepper, and ⅛ teaspoon *pepper* in a large saucepan.

- Bring mixture to boiling; reduce heat. Cover and simmer for 20 minutes. To serve, ladle soup into soup bowls. Dollop *each* serving with *1 tablespoon* of the plain yogurt. Makes 4 servings.

Minestrone

Per serving:
241 cal. (11% from fat), 17 g pro., 43 g carbo., 3 g fat,
3 mg cholesterol, 9 g dietary fiber, 1,308 mg sodium.

Preparation time:
15 minutes

Cooking time:
30 minutes

If you're watching your sodium as well as your fat, you might want to use low-sodium chicken broth in place of the regular chicken broth. The low-sodium product has one-third less sodium.

1 cup chopped onion

½ cup chopped carrot

½ cup sliced celery

1 16-ounce can tomatoes

2 14½-ounce cans chicken or beef broth

1 cup shredded cabbage

¾ cup tomato juice

1 teaspoon dried basil, crushed

¼ teaspoon garlic powder

1 15-ounce can cannellini or great northern beans

1 medium zucchini, sliced

½ of a 9-ounce package frozen Italian-style green beans

½ cup broken spaghetti

2 tablespoons grated Parmesan cheese

- Cook onion, carrot, and celery in small amount of water in a Dutch oven until tender; drain.

- Cut up tomatoes. Add *undrained* tomatoes, broth, cabbage, tomato juice, basil, and garlic powder to vegetables in Dutch oven. Bring to boiling; reduce heat. Cover and simmer for 20 minutes.

- Rinse and drain cannellini or great northern beans. Stir cannellini or great northern beans, zucchini, green beans, and spaghetti into mixture in Dutch oven. Return to boiling; reduce heat. Cover and simmer 10 to 15 minutes or until vegetables and pasta are tender. Pass Parmesan cheese to sprinkle on soup. Makes 4 servings.

Side Dishes

Vegetables, rice, pastas, and breads are perfect partners in your low-fat lifestyle. They're all satisfyingly filling, yet naturally low in fat. And as long as you enjoy them without high-fat seasonings, sauces, and spreads, you're sure to keep your healthful diet tastily on track.

Fresh-Greens Salad with Savory Dressings (See recipe, page 62.)

Spanish Rice

Per serving:
110 cal. (4% from fat), 3 g pro., 24 g carbo., 0 g fat,
0 mg cholesterol, 2 g dietary fiber, 304 mg sodium.

Preparation time:
10 minutes

Cooking time:
25 minutes

This spicy tomato-and-rice dish goes great with broiled chicken or fish. Add steamed broccoli or asparagus spears as a vegetable accompaniment.

1	cup water
¾	cup chopped green pepper
½	cup chopped onion
½	cup chopped celery
½	teaspoon salt
1	14½-ounce can tomatoes, cut up
¾	cup long-grain rice
1	teaspoon chili powder
⅛	teaspoon ground black pepper
	Dash bottled hot pepper sauce

- Combine water, green pepper, onion, celery, and salt in a medium saucepan. Bring to boiling; reduce heat. Cover and simmer for 5 minutes.

- Stir in *undrained* tomatoes, *uncooked* rice, chili powder, ground pepper, and hot pepper sauce. Return to boiling; reduce heat. Cover and simmer about 20 minutes or until rice is tender and liquid is absorbed. Serves 6.

Lemony Rice and Vegetables

Per serving:
107 cal. (5% from fat), 4 g pro., 21 g carbo., 1 g fat,
0 mg cholesterol, 2 g dietary fiber, 224 mg sodium.

Preparation time:
10 minutes

Cooking time:
20 minutes

The cumin gives this recipe a hint of Tex-Mex flavor. The lemon gives it a touch of freshness.

1¼	cups chicken broth
½	cup long-grain rice
¼	teaspoon ground cumin
⅛	teaspoon ground black pepper
1	small green or red sweet pepper, chopped
¼	cup sliced green onions
1	cup frozen peas
2	tablespoons snipped fresh parsley
1	teaspoon finely shredded lemon peel

- Heat chicken broth to boiling in a saucepan. Stir in *uncooked* rice, cumin, and ground pepper. Cover and simmer for 10 minutes.

- Stir in sweet pepper and green onions; return to boiling. Cover and cook about 10 minutes more or until rice is tender. Stir in peas, parsley, and lemon peel; heat through. Makes 5 servings.

Herbed Couscous and Vegetables

Per serving:
135 cal. (20% from fat), 4 g pro., 24 g carbo., 3 g fat,
0 mg cholesterol, 4 g dietary fiber, 165 mg sodium.

Preparation time:
10 minutes

Cooking time:
8 minutes

Standing time:
5 minutes

This savory dish, reminiscent of rice pilaf, uses couscous. You'll find this grain product, a traditional favorite in North African cooking, in the rice or pasta section of the supermarket.

1   tablespoon margarine

1   cup sliced fresh mushrooms

1   cup water

1   tablespoon snipped fresh parsley

½   teaspoon dried basil, crushed

¼   teaspoon salt

⅛   teaspoon dried oregano, crushed

    Dash pepper

⅔   cup couscous

1   medium tomato, peeled, seeded, and chopped

• Melt margarine in a medium saucepan. Add mushrooms and cook until tender.

• Carefully add water to saucepan. Stir in parsley, basil, salt, oregano, and pepper. Bring to boiling; remove from heat. Stir in couscous.

• Let stand, covered, for 5 minutes. Stir in chopped tomato. Makes 4 servings.

Vegetables and Fettuccine

Per serving:
163 cal. (21% from fat), 4 g pro., 28 g carbo., 4 g fat,
4 mg cholesterol, 2 g dietary fiber, 366 mg sodium.

Preparation time:
20 minutes

Cooking time:
8 minutes

Sliced fresh mushrooms, onion, and zucchini dress up meatless spaghetti sauce without adding any fat. This tasty side dish is great served with broiled chicken breasts.

4   ounces fettuccine

1   cup sliced fresh mushrooms

¼   cup chopped onion

2   tablespoons dry red wine or water

½   of a medium zucchini, sliced

1   15½-ounce jar regular or lower-fat meatless spaghetti sauce

2   tablespoons snipped fresh parsley

½   teaspoon bottled minced garlic or ⅛ teaspoon garlic powder

• Cook pasta according to package directions. Drain.

• Meanwhile, combine mushrooms, onion, and wine or water in a medium saucepan. Cook, uncovered, over medium-high heat about 3 minutes or until tender. Add zucchini, spaghetti sauce, parsley, and garlic. Bring to boiling; reduce heat. Simmer, uncovered, about 5 minutes or until zucchini is tender.

• Transfer pasta to a large serving bowl. Pour sauce over pasta. Toss lightly until coated. Makes 6 servings.

Tomato-Pepper Fettuccine

Tomato-Pepper Fettuccine

Per serving:
207 cal. (12% from fat), 7 g pro., 39 g carbo., 3 g fat,
0 mg cholesterol, 4 g dietary fiber, 80 mg sodium.

Preparation time:
10 minutes

Cooking time:
5 minutes

The Tupperware® Meals in Minutes™ microsteamer is ideal for microwave cooking this easy pasta recipe. Or, you can prepare the dish on the rangetop.

2 ounces refrigerated spinach fettuccine, cut into 3-inch pieces

⅔ cup water

1 tablespoon snipped fresh oregano or ½ teaspoon dried oregano, crushed

½ teaspoon cooking oil

1 small yellow sweet pepper, cut into strips

6 cherry tomatoes, halved

1 tablespoon lower-calorie Italian salad dressing

- Combine fettuccine, water, oregano, and oil in Meals in Minutes™ microsteamer dish. Arrange pepper strips in Colander. Place Colander in Dish. Cover and cook on 100 percent power (high) 5 to 7 minutes or until fettuccine is just tender, turning Dish once. Drain fettuccine over pepper strips; return all to Dish. Stir in tomatoes and salad dressing. Garnish with cherry tomato halves, fresh parsley, and fresh rosemary, if desired. Makes 2 servings.

Conventional Cooking Directions: Bring water to boiling in a medium saucepan. Add fettuccine, oregano, cooking oil, and pepper strips. Return to boiling; reduce heat. Simmer, covered, 2 to 3 minutes or until fettuccine is just tender. Drain. Stir in tomatoes and salad dressing.

Spaghetti with Cottage Cheese Pesto

Per serving:
150 cal. (14% from fat), 7 g pro., 25 g carbo., 2 g fat,
2 mg cholesterol, 1 g dietary fiber, 100 mg sodium.

Preparation time:
15 minutes

Cooking time:
8 minutes

This variation of pesto has no nuts and less oil than traditional pesto, so the fat is reduced by one-third. A Tupperware® 4¾-ounce Freezer Mates® container is just the right size for freezing the extra pesto. For best flavor, use the frozen pesto within two months.

1 10-ounce package frozen chopped spinach, thawed and well drained

½ cup hot water

⅓ cup low-fat cottage cheese

⅓ cup snipped fresh basil or 2 tablespoons dried basil, crushed

2 tablespoons grated Parmesan cheese

2 teaspoons olive oil or cooking oil

2 cloves garlic, minced

4 ounces spaghetti or fusilli, cooked and drained

- For pesto, combine spinach, water, cottage cheese, basil, Parmesan cheese, oil, and garlic in a blender container or food processor bowl. Cover and blend or process until smooth.

- Spoon *half* of the pesto (about ½ cup) over the hot, cooked pasta. Toss to mix well. Serve immediately. Makes 4 servings.

Note: Seal, label, and freeze the remaining pesto. To serve, thaw the pesto in the refrigerator. Place in a small saucepan and heat over low heat. Toss pesto with another 4 ounces of spaghetti or fusilli, cooked and drained. Makes 4 servings.

Zucchini-Wheat Muffins

Per muffin:
110 cal. (30% from fat), 3 g pro., 17 g carbo., 4 g fat,
0 mg cholesterol, 2 g dietary fiber, 92 mg sodium.

Preparation time:
15 minutes

Baking time:
15 minutes

Make and freeze a batch of these muffins. It takes just 30 seconds to warm one for breakfast, using the 100 percent power (high) setting on your microwave oven.

¾ cup whole wheat flour

¼ cup all-purpose flour

3 tablespoons sugar

1 teaspoon baking powder

⅛ teaspoon salt

⅓ cup skim milk

2 egg whites

2 tablespoons cooking oil

½ teaspoon finely shredded orange peel

¼ of a small zucchini

Nonstick spray coating

- Stir together whole wheat flour, all-purpose flour, sugar, baking powder, and salt.

- Use a fork to beat together milk, egg whites, oil, and orange peel. Shred zucchini (you should have about ½ cup). Add zucchini to milk mixture.

- Add zucchini mixture to flour mixture; stir just until moistened (batter should be lumpy). Spray cold muffin cups with nonstick coating. Fill cups half full. Bake in a 400° oven for 15 to 20 minutes or until golden brown.

- Remove muffins from cups; cool on wire rack. Makes 8 muffins.

Apple-and-Oat Bran Muffins

Per muffin:
113 cal. (23% from fat), 4 g pro., 20 g carbo., 3 g fat,
1 mg cholesterol, 3 g dietary fiber, 160 mg sodium.

Preparation time:
12 minutes

Baking time:
18 minutes

Nothing is more tempting than muffins straight from the oven. This easy recipe combines the spicy goodness of nutmeg and cinnamon with apple and wholesome oat bran. Look for oat bran in the cereal section of the supermarket.

1¼ cups whole wheat flour

1 cup oat bran

⅓ cup packed brown sugar

2½ teaspoons baking powder

¼ teaspoon baking soda

¼ teaspoon ground nutmeg

¼ teaspoon ground cinnamon

1 cup buttermilk or sour milk*

2 egg whites

2 tablespoons cooking oil

¾ cup shredded peeled apple

Nonstick spray coating

- Stir together whole wheat flour, oat bran, brown sugar, baking powder, baking soda, nutmeg, cinnamon, and ¼ teaspoon *salt* in a medium bowl. Set aside.

- Combine buttermilk, egg whites, and oil in a small bowl. Add to dry ingredients; stir just until moistened. Stir in shredded apple. Store batter, tightly covered, in the refrigerator for up to 5 days.

- To bake muffins, spray cold muffin cups with nonstick coating. Spoon about ¼ *cup* batter into *each* muffin cup. Bake in a 375° oven for 18 to 20 minutes or until a wooden toothpick inserted near the centers comes out clean. Serve warm. Makes 12 muffins.

*To make sour milk, use 1 tablespoon *lemon juice* or *vinegar* plus enough *whole milk* to make 1 cup; let stand 5 minutes before using.

Carrots and Pea Pods in Orange Sauce

Per serving:
60 cal. (3% from fat), 3 g pro., 12 g carbo., 0 g fat,
0 mg cholesterol, 3 g dietary fiber, 219 mg sodium.

Preparation time:
10 minutes

Cooking time:
15 minutes

The orange sauce gives the vegetables a golden glaze and an Oriental flavor. The sauce also would taste great with cauliflower or green beans.

1 cup bias-sliced carrots

2 cups fresh pea pods or one 6-ounce package frozen pea pods

½ teaspoon finely shredded orange peel (set aside)

⅓ cup orange juice

1 teaspoon cornstarch

2 teaspoons soy sauce

- Cook carrots in a small amount of boiling salted water in a covered medium saucepan for 5 minutes. Add fresh or frozen pea pods. Cook 2 to 4 minutes more or until vegetables are crisp-tender. Drain; return vegetables to saucepan. Cover to keep warm.

- Meanwhile, for sauce, combine orange juice and cornstarch in a small saucepan. Cook and stir over medium heat until mixture is thickened and bubbly. Cook and stir 2 minutes more. Stir in orange peel and soy sauce. Pour sauce over vegetables and toss. Makes 4 servings.

Creamy Potato Salad

Per serving:
116 cal. (2% from fat), 4 g pro., 26 g carbo., 0 g fat,
0 mg cholesterol, 2 g dietary fiber, 288 mg sodium.

Preparation time:
30 minutes

Chilling time:
6 hours

Without regular mayonnaise, whole milk, and egg yolks, this picnic-time favorite loses most of its fat and cholesterol.

3 medium potatoes (1 pound total)

⅓ cup nonfat mayonnaise or salad dressing

¼ cup thinly sliced celery

¼ cup chopped green pepper

2 tablespoons chopped onion

2 tablespoons skim milk

1 teaspoon prepared mustard

1 teaspoon vinegar

⅛ teaspoon salt

⅛ teaspoon pepper

2 hard-cooked egg whites, coarsely chopped

Skim milk

- Cook potatoes in boiling water in a covered saucepan for 20 to 25 minutes or until just tender. Drain well. Peel and cube potatoes.

- Stir together mayonnaise or salad dressing, celery, green pepper, onion, the 2 tablespoons milk, the mustard, vinegar, salt, and pepper in a large salad bowl. Add cooked potatoes and egg whites. Toss lightly to mix.

- Cover and chill for 6 to 24 hours. If necessary, stir in a little additional milk before serving to make the salad of desired consistency. Makes 4 servings.

Oriental Rice Salad

Oriental Rice Salad

Per serving:
93 cal. (18% from fat), 3 g pro., 17 g carbo., 2 g fat,
0 mg cholesterol, 2 g dietary fiber, 166 mg sodium.

Preparation time:
15 minutes

Cooking time:
45 minutes

Standing time:
10 minutes

Chilling time:
3 hours

"Delicious!" is how one of our tasters described this salad with a slightly nutty flavor. Rice vinegar gives the slightly sweet dressing a milder flavor than cider or white vinegar.

⅓ cup wild rice

1¾ cups water

⅛ teaspoon salt

⅓ cup long-grain rice

¼ cup shredded carrot

2 tablespoons rice vinegar or vinegar

1 tablespoon salad oil

1 tablespoon soy sauce

2 teaspoons honey

½ teaspoon grated fresh gingerroot or ¼ teaspoon ground ginger

1 cup fresh pea pods or one 6-ounce package frozen pea pods, thawed

½ cup chopped water chestnuts

- Rinse wild rice under cold running water about 1 minute. Bring the wild rice, water, and salt to boiling in a small saucepan. Reduce heat. Cover and simmer for 30 minutes.

- Stir in the long-grain rice and carrot. Return to boiling; reduce heat. Cover and simmer about 15 minutes more or until water is absorbed and rice is just done. Remove from heat. Let stand, covered, 10 minutes.

- For dressing, combine vinegar, oil, soy sauce, honey, and gingerroot or ginger in a Tupperware® Modular Mates® Round 1 container. Apply seal and shake well. Transfer rice mixture to the Tupperware 6½-cup Serving Bowl. Pour dressing over rice mixture. Toss to coat. Cover and chill 3 to 24 hours.

- Just before serving, stir in pea pods and water chestnuts. Makes 8 servings.

Sodium Sense

Since you're already watching the fat in your diet as part of a healthy lifestyle, you may want to keep track of the sodium in your food as well. Here's the first step. Begin using as many of the sodium-reduced products—including canned tomatoes, tomato juice, canned tuna, soy sauce, and cheese—as you can. For help reading the labels of these foods, keep this list of sodium-related terms in mind.

Sodium-free: A product that contains no more than 5 milligrams of sodium per serving.

Very-low-sodium: A product that has no more than 35 milligrams of sodium per serving.

Low-sodium A food that contains no more than 140 milligrams of sodium per serving.

Reduced-sodium: A food in which the sodium level has been reduced by at least 75 percent from the original product.

No-salt-added: A food to which the processor has not added any salt. However, remember that the food already may be naturally high in sodium.

Fresh-Greens Salad with Savory Dressings

Per serving:
53 cal. (22% from fat), 2 g pro., 9 g carbo., 1 g fat,
0 mg cholesterol, 3 g dietary fiber, 58 mg sodium.

**Preparation time:
25 minutes**

Jicama is a large brown root vegetable that peels and cuts easily to give crisp, white pieces—perfect for salads, such as this one.

12 cups torn mixed salad greens

2 cups jicama, cut into julienne strips

1½ cups fresh pea pods

2 oranges, peeled and sliced

1 medium cucumber, thinly sliced

Avocado-Yogurt Dressing (see recipe at right)

Creamy Basil Dressing (see recipe at right)

● Place greens in the Watercolor® salad bowl. Arrange jicama, pea pods, oranges, and cucumber over greens. Prepare Avocado-Yogurt Dressing; spoon into one of the compartments of the Watercolor® dip container. Prepare Creamy Basil Dressing; spoon into remaining compartment of the dip container. Makes 12 servings.

Avocado-Yogurt Dressing: Halve and remove seed from 1 small *avocado*. Peel *half* of the avocado and place in a blender container or food processor bowl. (Reserve remaining half for another use.) Add ⅓ cup *plain nonfat yogurt*, ½ of a small *onion* (cut up), 1 tablespoon *skim milk*, ½ teaspoon finely shredded *lemon peel*, ¼ teaspoon *salt*, ¼ teaspoon finely shredded *orange peel*, ⅛ teaspoon *garlic powder*, and dash *ground red pepper*. Cover and blend or process until smooth. Makes about ¾ cup (six 2-tablespoon servings).

Creamy Basil Dressing: Stir together ⅓ cup *nonfat mayonnaise* or *salad dressing*, ¼ cup *buttermilk*, and ¾ teaspoon snipped *fresh basil* or ¼ teaspoon *dried basil*, crushed, in a bowl. If necessary, stir in enough *skim milk* (1 to 2 teaspoons) to make of desired consistency. Makes about ¾ cup (six 2-tablespoon servings).

Note: Pictured on pages 52–53.

Oh-So-Easy Oil-Free Dressing

You can turn any salad from high-fat to low-fat with this delicious no-oil vinaigrette dressing. The fruit pectin gives this salad dressing body without using oil.

Oil-Free Salad Dressing: Combine 1 tablespoon *powdered fruit pectin*, ½ teaspoon *sugar*, ¼ teaspoon dried crushed *basil*, ⅛ teaspoon *dry mustard*, and ⅛ teaspoon *garlic powder* in a small mixing bowl. Stir in ¼ cup *water* and 1 tablespoon *red wine vinegar*. Cover and chill the dressing at least 1 hour. Serve over your favorite combination of salad greens and vegetables. Store any remaining dressing in the refrigerator for up to 3 days. Makes 6 (4-teaspoon) servings.

Per serving: 9 cal. (0% from fat), 0 g pro., 2 g carbo., 0 g fat,
0 mg cholesterol, 0 g dietary fiber, 1 mg sodium.

Citrus Coleslaw

Per serving:
71 cal. (6% from fat), 3 g pro., 15 g carbo., 1 g fat,
1 mg cholesterol, 2 g dietary fiber, 34 mg sodium.

Preparation time:
10 minutes

Serve this refreshing side-dish salad with grilled chicken sandwiches and steamed asparagus or green beans for an easy weeknight supper.

½ cup orange low-fat yogurt

1 tablespoon skim milk

⅛ teaspoon ground ginger

3 cups shredded coleslaw mix or 3 cups shredded cabbage and grated carrot

1 11-ounce can mandarin orange sections, chilled and drained, or 1 cup fresh orange sections, drained

- For dressing, combine orange yogurt, skim milk, and ground ginger in a medium mixing bowl. Combine well.

- Add coleslaw mix or shredded cabbage and grated carrot and orange sections to yogurt mixture; toss to coat with dressing. Makes 4 servings.

Fruit Salad with Poppy-Seed Dressing

Per serving:
99 cal. (7% from fat), 2 g pro., 23 g carbo., 1 g fat,
1 mg cholesterol, 3 g dietary fiber, 23 mg sodium.

Preparation time:
15 minutes

Next time, vary the kinds of fresh fruits you use. Try blueberries and pears in place of the strawberries and apple.

1 8-ounce can pineapple tidbits (juice pack)

1½ cups small strawberries or seedless red grapes

1 medium apple, cored and cut into bite-size pieces

1 11-ounce can mandarin orange sections, drained

½ cup pineapple low-fat yogurt

½ teaspoon poppy seed

Lettuce leaves

- Drain pineapple, reserving *1 tablespoon* of the juice. If using strawberries, cut berries in half.

- For the fruit mixture, combine pineapple tidbits, strawberries or grapes, apple pieces, and orange sections in a medium mixing bowl. Toss lightly to mix.

- For dressing, combine yogurt, poppy seed, and the reserved pineapple juice.

- To serve, line salad plates with the lettuce leaves. Arrange fruit mixture on lettuce. Drizzle dressing over fruit. Makes 5 or 6 servings.

Vegetable-Tortellini Soup

Garden Bounty Casserole

Per serving:
156 cal. (27% from fat), 7 g pro., 23 g carbo., 5 g fat,
13 mg cholesterol, 5 g dietary fiber, 142 mg sodium.

Preparation time:
15 minutes

Cooking time:
23 minutes

For added bite, use Monterey Jack cheese with jalapeño peppers.

½	pound green, yellow wax, or purple beans, cleaned
2	medium carrots
2	medium ears of corn
¼	cup water
¾	cup shredded Monterey Jack cheese (3 ounces)
½	cup couscous
¼	cup milk
⅛	teaspoon salt
⅛	teaspoon pepper

- Bias-cut beans into 1-inch pieces. Thinly bias-slice carrots. Cut corn from cobs.

- Combine bias-cut beans and the water in a medium saucepan; cover and cook 10 minutes. Add bias-sliced carrots and the corn. Cook, covered, 8 to 10 minutes more or until nearly tender. Stir in ½ cup of the cheese, the couscous, milk, salt, and pepper.

- Cook, covered, on low heat 5 minutes or until vegetables are crisp-tender, stirring once. Sprinkle remaining cheese on top. Makes 6 servings.

Microwave Cooking Directions: Cut vegetables as directed above. Combine beans and the water in a Tupperware® 1¾-quart TupperWave® casserole. Micro-cook, covered, on 100 percent power (high) 4 minutes, stirring once. Add carrots and corn. Cook, covered, on high 5 minutes, stirring once. Stir in ½ cup of the cheese, the couscous, milk, salt, and pepper. Cook, covered, on high 3 to 4 minutes or until vegetables are crisp-tender; stir once. Sprinkle with remaining cheese.

Vegetable-Tortellini Soup

Per serving:
81 cal. (13% from fat), 4 g pro., 14 g carbo., 1 g fat,
11 mg cholesterol, 2 g dietary fiber, 883 mg sodium.

Preparation time:
5 minutes

Cooking time:
10 minutes

If you can't find frozen tortellini, use refrigerated tortellini instead. Check the cooking directions on the package; you'll need to add the refrigerated tortellini later, so it cooks only for the time recommended.

3	cups water
1	tablespoon instant beef bouillon granules
½	teaspoon dried basil, crushed
¼	teaspoon dried oregano, crushed
½	cup thinly sliced carrots
½	cup frozen cheese tortellini
1	8-ounce can tomatoes
1	small zucchini, halved lengthwise and thinly sliced
1	tablespoon snipped fresh parsley

- Combine water, bouillon granules, basil, and oregano in a medium saucepan. Bring to boiling. Stir in carrots and tortellini.

- Return to boiling; reduce heat. Simmer, uncovered, for 5 minutes. Add tomatoes and zucchini. Return to boiling; reduce heat. Simmer, uncovered, 3 to 5 minutes more or until vegetables and tortellini are tender. Stir in parsley. Makes 4 servings.

Herb Biscuits

Per serving:
57 cal. (22% from fat), 1 g pro., 10 g carbo., 1 g fat,
1 mg cholesterol, 0 g dietary fiber, 194 mg sodium.

Preparation time:
10 minutes

Baking time:
8 minutes

These savory, pull-apart biscuits are ideal to serve with a hearty soup or a chef's salad. You also can enjoy them as an appetizer or snack.

1   tablespoon grated Romano or Parmesan cheese

½   teaspoon dried basil or oregano, crushed

     Dash garlic powder

     Nonstick spray coating

1   4½-ounce package (6) refrigerated biscuits

1   tablespoon skim milk

- For herb mixture, combine cheese, basil or oregano, and garlic powder. Spray a 7½x3½x2-inch loaf pan with nonstick coating.

- Using kitchen shears, cut each biscuit into 4 pieces; arrange pieces randomly in the prepared pan. Brush pieces with milk; sprinkle with the herb mixture. Bake in a 450° oven 8 to 10 minutes or until golden brown. Makes 1 loaf (6 servings).

Dill Rolls

Per roll:
84 cal. (10% from fat), 5 g pro., 14 g carbo., 1 g fat,
19 mg cholesterol, 1 g dietary fiber, 171 mg sodium.

Preparation time:
20 minutes

Rising time:
1¼ hours

Resting time:
5 minutes

Baking time:
15 minutes

By using cottage cheese instead of shortening or cooking oil, you can cut down on the fat, yet still achieve a tender and moist bread.

1½ cups all-purpose flour

1   package active dry yeast

1   cup low-fat cottage cheese

¼   cup water

1   tablespoon sugar

2   teaspoons dillseed or caraway seed

½   teaspoon salt

1   egg

     Nonstick spray coating

- Combine *1 cup* of the flour and the yeast in a small mixing bowl. Heat and stir cottage cheese, water, sugar, dillseed or caraway seed, and salt in a small saucepan just until warm (120° to 130°). Add to flour mixture along with egg.

- Beat on low speed of an electric mixer for 30 seconds, scraping bowl constantly. Beat mixture on high speed for 3 minutes.

- Add the remaining flour; beat on low speed about 2 minutes or until nearly smooth. Cover batter and let rise in a warm place until double (about 45 minutes). Stir batter down with a wooden spoon. Let rest for 5 minutes.

- Spray 12 cold muffin cups with nonstick coating. Spoon batter evenly into cups. Cover loosely with waxed paper; let batter rise until nearly double (about 30 minutes).

- Bake in a 375° oven for 15 to 18 minutes or until golden brown. Serve warm. Makes 12 rolls.

Barley-Wheat Bread

Per serving:
137 cal. (15% from fat), 5 g pro., 25 g carbo., 2 g fat,
14 mg cholesterol, 2 g dietary fiber, 146 mg sodium.

Preparation time:
40 minutes

Rising time:
2 hours

Resting time:
10 minutes

Baking time:
35 minutes

Barley and oats give this bread a unique texture and flavor. Try it toasted and spread with your favorite all-fruit preserves.

½ cup quick-cooking barley

3¾ to 4 cups all-purpose flour

2 packages active dry yeast

1 cup low-fat cottage cheese

1 cup water

½ cup honey

¼ cup margarine

1½ teaspoons salt

2 eggs

2½ cups whole wheat flour

½ cup quick-cooking rolled oats

● Cook barley according to the package directions; drain well.

● Combine *2 cups* of the all-purpose flour and the yeast in a large mixing bowl.

● Heat and stir cottage cheese, water, honey, margarine, and salt in a saucepan just until warm (120° to 130°) and margarine is almost melted. Add to flour mixture.

● Add eggs; beat on low speed of an electric mixer for 30 seconds, scraping bowl constantly. Beat on high speed for 3 minutes. Using a spoon, stir in barley, whole wheat flour, oats, and as much of the remaining all-purpose flour as you can.

● Turn dough out onto a lightly floured surface. Knead in enough of the remaining all-purpose flour to make a stiff dough that is smooth and elastic (8 to 10 minutes total). Shape into a ball. Place in a greased bowl; turn to grease surface. Cover; let rise in a warm place until nearly double (about 1¼ hours).

● Punch dough down; turn out onto a floured surface. Divide in half; shape into two balls. Cover; let rest 10 minutes. Shape each ball of dough into a loaf; place in two greased 9x5x3-inch loaf pans. Cover; let rise in a warm place until nearly double (45 to 60 minutes).

● Bake in a 350° oven for 35 to 40 minutes or until bread tests done. (Cover with foil after 25 minutes to prevent overbrowning.) Remove from pans; cool on a wire rack. Makes 2 loaves (32 servings).

Cottage Cheese Choices

You may think that all cottage cheeses are alike, but from a fat standpoint, there are differences. Buying the wrong type can increase the fat content of a recipe quite a bit. Here's what you'll find in the dairy case.

Creamed cottage cheese is the richest and creamiest. It contains 4 percent or more milk fat and has about 110 calories and 5 grams of fat in a ½-cup serving.

Low-fat cottage cheese is the most popular choice for low-fat cooking. It contains not less that ½ percent and not more than 2 percent milk fat. Low-fat cottage cheese with 2 percent milk fat has about 105 calories and 2 grams of fat in a ½-cup serving. Low-fat cottage cheese with 1 percent milk fat has about 85 calories and 1 gram of fat in a ½-cup serving.

Dry-curd cottage cheese contains no added cream and has less than ½ percent milk fat. It has about 65 calories and less than 1 gram of fat in a ½-cup serving.

Four-Grain Bread

Four-Grain Bread

Per serving:
62 cal. (20% from fat), 2 g pro., 11 g carbo., 1 g fat,
8 mg cholesterol, 1 g dietary fiber, 78 mg sodium.

Preparation time:
30 minutes

Rising time:
1¾ hours

Resting time:
10 minutes

Baking time:
30 minutes

This whole-grain loaf is formed in a classic Italian bread shape, one that resembles the top of a wheat stalk. You can re-create this impressive shaping if you follow the directions in the tip below.

1¾ to 2¼ cups all-purpose flour

1 package active dry yeast

¾ cup milk

3 tablespoons honey

2 tablespoons shortening or margarine

1 teaspoon salt

1 egg

⅓ cup whole wheat flour

3 tablespoons rye flour

3 tablespoons quick-cooking rolled oats

3 tablespoons toasted wheat germ

1 tablespoon cornmeal

1 beaten egg white

- Combine *1 cup* of the all-purpose flour and the yeast in a medium mixing bowl; set aside.

- Heat and stir milk, honey, shortening, and salt in a small saucepan just until warm (120° to 130°) and shortening almost melts. Add to flour mixture in bowl. Add egg. Beat on medium speed of an electric mixer for 30 seconds, scraping bowl constantly. Beat on high speed 3 minutes. Using a spoon, stir in whole wheat and rye flours, oats, wheat germ, and cornmeal. Then, stir in as much of the remaining all-purpose flour as you can.

- Turn dough out onto a lightly floured surface. Knead in enough of the remaining all-purpose flour to make a moderately stiff dough that is smooth and elastic (6 to 8 minutes total). Shape into a ball. Place in a greased bowl; turn once. Cover and let rise in warm place until double (1 to 1½ hours). Punch dough down. Cover; let rest 10 minutes.

- Refer to the tip below for shaping dough.

- Bake in a 375° oven for 30 to 35 minutes or until done. (Cover with foil after 20 minutes.) Remove from pan and cool on a wire rack. Store in the Tupperware® Jumbo Bread Server. Makes 1 loaf (12 servings).

Shaping It Right

To shape Four-Grain Bread into a beautiful work of art, just follow these steps.

- Grease a baking sheet and sprinkle with additional wheat germ, cornmeal, or rolled oats; set aside.
- Turn the dough out onto a lightly floured surface. Set aside one-third of the dough.
- Shape the remaining dough into an oval about 11 inches long and 3 inches wide. Place on the prepared baking sheet.
- Using a sharp knife, score the dough deeply around the entire oval about ¾ inch from outside edge. Using kitchen shears, make diagonal cuts around the edge of the dough about 1½ inches apart, cutting to the scored line and angling all cuts toward one end of the loaf to create a feathered look.
- Repeat with reserved dough, *except* start with a 10x2-inch oval, score ½ inch from edge, and make diagonal cuts 1 inch apart.
- Brush the larger oval with some of the beaten egg white. Set the smaller oval on top of the larger oval. Cover and let rise until nearly double (45 to 60 minutes).
- Brush the tops of the ovals with the remaining egg white. If desired, sprinkle with sesame seed, poppy seed, and/or toasted wheat germ. Then bake as directed above.

Desserts

Yes, you *can* have your cake and eat low-fat, too! You also can have your cobbler, your custard, your cheesecake, and any of our other delectable desserts. They're all designed to give a happy ending to any low-fat meal.

Dutch Babies with Fresh Fruit
(See recipe, page 72.)

Dutch Babies with Fresh Fruit

Per serving:
173 cal. (19% from fat), 6 g pro., 30 g carbo., 4 g fat,
36 mg cholesterol, 2 g dietary fiber, 108 mg sodium.

Preparation time:
15 minutes

Baking time:
15 minutes

This unique dessert blends the airy lightness of popoverlike Dutch Babies with the wonderful flavor of fresh fruit. Try a mixture of sliced strawberries, nectarines, kiwi fruit, and/or whole raspberries, blueberries, and boysen-berries, or use your favorite fruit all by itself. Either way, you'll love the delicious results!

Nonstick spray coating

4 egg whites

1 egg

½ cup all-purpose flour

½ cup skim milk

1 tablespoon cooking oil

¼ teaspoon ground nutmeg

¼ teaspoon almond extract

⅛ teaspoon salt

¼ cup reduced-calorie orange marmalade or orange marmalade

4 cups mixed fresh fruit

1 teaspoon lemon juice

Whipped Topper (see tip, below) or powdered sugar (optional)

- Generously spray nonstick coating on the bottom and up sides of six 4½-inch pie plates or 4½-inch foil tart pans.

- Beat egg whites and egg in a medium mixing bowl with a rotary beater or whisk until combined. Add flour, milk, oil, nutmeg, almond extract, and salt. Beat until smooth.

- Divide batter among prepared pans. Bake in a 400° oven for 15 to 20 minutes or until golden brown and puffy.

- Melt marmalade in a medium saucepan; cool slightly. Gently stir in fruit and lemon juice.

- Immediately after removing popover tarts from oven, transfer to a serving platter. Spoon some of the fruit mixture into the center of each tart. If desired, spoon Whipped Topper onto tarts or lightly sift powdered sugar over tarts. Serve tarts immediately. Makes 6 servings.

Note: Pictured on pages 70–71.

Low-Fat and Luscious

For those desserts that just wouldn't be the same without a spoonful of whipped cream, try this delicious low-fat alternative.

Whipped Topper: Combine 2 tablespoons *ice water*, 1½ teaspoons *orange juice*, and ¼ teaspoon *vanilla* in a small mixing bowl. Stir in 3 tablespoons *nonfat dry milk powder*. Beat with an electric mixer on high speed for 3 to 6 minutes or until soft peaks form (tips curl). Add 1 tablespoon *sugar* and beat 1 minute more. Serve immediately. Makes ¾ cup topping (six 2-tablespoon servings).

Per serving: 16 cal. (1% from fat), 1 g pro., 3 g carbo., 0 g fat, 0 mg cholesterol, 0 g dietary fiber, 12 mg sodium.

Note: Whenever you need more servings of topping, just double the recipe.

Baked Apples with Cheese Topping

Per serving:
132 cal. (22% from fat), 2 g pro., 26 g carbo., 3 g fat,
10 mg cholesterol, 3 g dietary fiber, 60 mg sodium.

Preparation time:
12 minutes

Baking time:
40 minutes

When making this recipe, be sure to snip your own dates. The pre-snipped dates available in stores have added sugar, which prevents them from sticking together but increases the calories.

4	small apples, cored (about 4 ounces each)
¼	cup snipped pitted whole dates or raisins
¼	cup water
2	ounces light cream cheese (Neufchâtel)
½	teaspoon vanilla
3	to 4 teaspoons skim milk
	Ground nutmeg or ground cinnamon

- Cut off a strip of peel from the top of each apple. Arrange apples in a 9-inch pie plate. Fill centers of apples with dates or raisins. Add water to pie plate. Bake, covered, in a 350° oven for 40 minutes or until tender. Cool slightly.

- Meanwhile, for topping, stir together cream cheese and vanilla in a small mixing bowl. Stir in enough skim milk to make topping of desired consistency.

- To serve, top the slightly cooled apples with some of the topping. Sprinkle lightly with nutmeg or cinnamon. Makes 4 servings.

Microwave Cooking Directions: Prepare as above, *except* arrange apples in a microwave-safe dish, such as the Tupperware® 1-quart TupperWave® casserole. Add the water to casserole. Cover with waxed paper. Micro-cook on 100 percent power (high) for 3 to 7 minutes or until tender, rearranging once. Continue with cream cheese topping as directed above.

Blueberry Parfaits

Per serving:
95 cal. (21% from fat), 2 g pro., 18 g carbo., 2 g fat,
7 mg cholesterol, 3 g dietary fiber, 41 mg sodium.

Preparation time:
15 minutes

Chilling time:
8 minutes

This star-spangled treat is ready in 23 minutes and has only 96 calories per serving.

3	tablespoons sugar
2	teaspoons cornstarch
1	cup fresh or frozen blueberries
⅓	cup orange juice
2	ounces light cream cheese (Neufchâtel)
1	tablespoon powdered sugar
2	teaspoons skim milk
2	cups fresh or frozen unsweetened red raspberries
	Orange peel twists (optional)

- Combine sugar and cornstarch in a small saucepan. Stir in ½ cup of the blueberries and the orange juice. Cook and stir until mixture is thickened and bubbly; cook and stir 2 minutes more.

- Remove from heat and stir in remaining blueberries. Cover and chill in the refrigerator while preparing cheese mixture.

- Beat cream cheese in a small mixing bowl until softened. Beat in powdered sugar and skim milk.

- To serve, alternately layer raspberries and blueberry mixture in 6 dessert dishes. Drizzle some of the cream cheese mixture over each serving. Garnish with orange peel twists, if desired. Makes 6 servings.

Poached Pears with Raspberry Sauce

Lemon Torte
with Raspberries

Per serving:
79 cal. (4% from fat), 3 g pro., 17 g carbo., 0 g fat,
1 mg cholesterol, 1 g dietary fiber, 107 mg sodium.

Preparation time:
20 minutes

Chilling time:
5 hours

Another time, serve this luscious lemon torte with fresh blueberries or sliced fresh strawberries. It still will be low in calories and fat-free.

Nonstick spray coating

1 4-serving-size package low-calorie lemon-flavored gelatin

½ cup boiling water

½ of a 6-ounce can (⅓ cup) frozen lemonade concentrate, thawed

1 12-ounce can evaporated skim milk

2 cups cubed angel food cake

2 cups fresh or frozen unsweetened raspberries

1 tablespoon sugar

- Spray the bottom only of an 8-inch springform pan with nonstick coating; set aside.

- Dissolve lemon gelatin in the boiling water in a large bowl. Stir in thawed lemonade concentrate and evaporated skim milk. Cover and chill in refrigerator for 1 to 1½ hours or until mixture mounds when spooned.

- After chilling, beat gelatin mixture with an electric mixer on medium to high speed for 5 to 6 minutes or until fluffy.

- Arrange angel food cake cubes in the bottom of the springform pan. Pour the chilled gelatin mixture over the cake cubes. Cover and chill in the refrigerator for 4 hours or until firm.

- Meanwhile, stir together raspberries and sugar in a small bowl. Cover and chill at least 2 hours.

- To serve, cut the torte into wedges and spoon the raspberry mixture on top. Makes 12 servings.

Poached Pears with
Raspberry Sauce

Per serving:
136 cal. (5% from fat), 1 g pro., 35 g carbo., 1 g fat,
0 mg cholesterol, 6 g dietary fiber, 0 mg sodium.

Preparation time:
20 minutes

Cooking time:
10 minutes

Chilling time:
3 hours

Make this dessert in summer and fall with Bartlett pears, and in winter with the Bosc variety. Both types are ideal for cooking because they hold their shape well.

6 firm ripe pears

4 cups water

¼ cup lemon juice

1 cup fresh or frozen unsweetened raspberries

⅓ cup orange juice

2 tablespoons sugar

2 teaspoons cornstarch

Low-fat vanilla yogurt (optional; see note)

- Peel pears, leaving stems intact. Cut a thin slice off one side of each pear so it will lie flat. Combine water and lemon juice in a large saucepan; bring to boiling. Add pears. Return to boiling; reduce heat and simmer, covered, for 10 to 15 minutes or until pears are tender. Drain. Place pears in a dish; cover. Chill 3 hours or overnight.

- Thaw raspberries, if frozen. Combine raspberries, orange juice, sugar, and cornstarch in a small saucepan. Cook and stir until thickened and bubbly; cook and stir 2 minutes more. Press through a fine sieve; discard seeds. Cover and chill until serving time.

- To serve, spoon chilled raspberry sauce into 6 individual dessert dishes. Place pears in sauce. Makes 6 servings.

Note: If desired, garnish the dessert by piping 3 drops of vanilla yogurt on top of sauce beside each pear. Run the tip of a knife through each drop, creating a heart shape, as shown.

Strawberry Shortcake

Per serving:
247 cal. (26% from fat), 5 g pro., 42 g carbo., 7 g fat,
0 mg cholesterol, 4 g dietary fiber, 198 mg sodium.

Preparation time:
15 minutes

Baking time:
10 minutes

Cooling time:
10 minutes

Make this summertime dessert by ladling lightly sweetened, fresh strawberries over shortcake. Our shortcake comes with less cholesterol and fat because we left out the egg.

3   cups sliced strawberries

2   tablespoons sugar

1   cup all-purpose flour

1   tablespoon sugar

1½ teaspoons baking powder

¼   teaspoon cream of tartar

⅛   teaspoon salt

2   tablespoons shortening

⅓   cup skim milk

Whipped Topper (see tip, page 72)

- Stir together *half* of the strawberries and the 2 tablespoons sugar in a medium mixing bowl. Mash strawberries slightly; set all berries aside.

- Stir together flour, the 1 tablespoon sugar, baking powder, cream of tartar, and salt in a medium mixing bowl. Using a pastry blender, cut in shortening until mixture resembles coarse crumbs. Make a well in center of dry ingredients; add milk all at once. Using a fork, stir just until dough clings together. Turn dough out onto a lightly floured surface. Quickly knead dough by gently folding and pressing the dough for 10 to 12 strokes. Pat or lightly roll dough to ½-inch thickness. Cut dough into 4 biscuits with a floured 2½-inch biscuit cutter, dipping the cutter into flour between cuts. Place biscuits on an ungreased baking sheet.

- Bake in a 450° oven for 10 minutes or until golden brown. Remove biscuits from the baking sheet and cool on a wire rack about 10 minutes.

- Meanwhile, fold remaining sliced strawberries into mashed berries. Split biscuits in half and spoon strawberry mixture between and over tops. Spoon on Whipped Topper. Serve immediately. Makes 4 servings.

Ice Cream Options

With all the various flavors and kinds of ice-creamlike treats to choose from, deciding what's best can be confusing. Here are just some of your low-fat options.

Ice milk: With 2 to 7 percent milk fat, ice milk closely resembles ice cream in flavor and texture, but it's not as rich.

Frozen yogurt: Without any federal standards, fat content can vary greatly among brands of frozen yogurt. Some brands taste much like ice cream and others do not. Be sure to read nutrition labels carefully for the fat content of the brands you are considering.

Sherbet: These fruit-flavored confections must contain from 1 to 2 percent milk fat by weight. In addition to some of the same ingredients used in ice creams and ice milks, sherbets contain varying amounts of fruit, fruit juices, and/or fruit flavors.

Lite ice-creamlike products: These products use fat substitutes to replace all or part of the milk fat used in regular ice creams and ice milks. Brands vary widely in their fat content, so be sure to read the nutrition label.

Fruit-Filled Meringue Shells

Per serving:
156 cal. (1% from fat), 2 g pro., 39 g carbo., 0 g fat,
0 mg cholesterol, 2 g dietary fiber, 17 mg sodium.

**Preparation time:
50 minutes**

**Baking time:
1 hour 35 minutes**

**Chilling time:
1 hour**

These dazzling individual desserts are derived from the Australian classic Pavlova, a crisp meringue shell filled with lots of fresh fruit, whipped cream, and a fruit sauce. To help lighten our version, we use a low-fat Whipped Topper instead of whipped cream.

2	egg whites
¾	teaspoon vanilla
¼	teaspoon cream of tartar
⅔	cup sugar
1	cup frozen unsweetened raspberries, thawed
2	tablespoons sugar
½	teaspoon cornstarch
3	cups peeled and sliced peaches or a combination of fresh fruit
	Whipped Topper (see tip, page 72)

- Place egg whites in a small mixing bowl and let stand at room temperature for 30 minutes. Meanwhile, cover a baking sheet with plain brown paper. Draw six 3-inch-diameter circles on the paper.

- For meringue, add vanilla and cream of tartar to egg whites. Beat with an electric mixer on medium speed until soft peaks form (tips curl). Add the ⅔ cup sugar, *1 tablespoon* at a time, beating on high speed until very stiff peaks form (tips stand straight) and sugar is almost dissolved (about 7 minutes).

- To make shells, pipe meringue through a pastry tube onto circles on the brown paper, building the sides up to form shells. (Or, use the back of a spoon to spread the meringue over the circles, building the sides up.)

- Bake in a 300° oven for 35 minutes. Turn off the oven and let dry in the oven, with the door closed, for 1 hour. Remove the meringue shells from the baking sheet. Cool thoroughly on a wire rack. Store in an airtight container until serving time.

- For raspberry sauce, puree berries in a blender container or food processor bowl, then press berries through a fine sieve. Discard seeds. (You should have about ⅓ cup puree.) Stir together the 2 tablespoons sugar and cornstarch in a saucepan. Add pureed berries. Cook and stir berry mixture until thickened and bubbly. Cook and stir 2 minutes more. Remove from heat. Cool sauce. Cover surface with waxed paper and chill sauce about 1 hour.

- Fill *each* meringue shell with ½ *cup* of the fruit mixture. Top with Whipped Topper and drizzle with raspberry sauce. Serve immediately. Makes 6 servings.

Chocolate-Cinnamon Angel Cake

Chocolate Sauce

Serve this irresistible low-fat chocolate sauce over frozen vanilla yogurt and fresh blueberries or sliced strawberries.

Chocolate Sauce: Mix 1½ cups *sugar*, ⅔ cup *unsweetened cocoa powder*, and 3 tablespoons *cornstarch* in a small saucepan. Stir in 1½ cups *evaporated skim milk*. Cook and stir until thickened and bubbly. Cook and stir 2 minutes more. Remove from heat. Stir in 2 teaspoons *vanilla*. Serve warm or cool. Cover and refrigerate any remaining sauce. Makes 16 (2-tablespoon) servings.

Per serving: 93 cal. (5% from fat), 1 g pro., 23 g carbo., 1 g fat, 0 mg cholesterol, 1 g dietary fiber, 12 mg sodium.

Chocolate-Cinnamon Angel Cake

Per serving:
374 cal. (4% from fat), 11 g pro., 83 g carbo., 2 g fat,
5 mg cholesterol, 2 g dietary fiber, 126 mg sodium.

**Preparation time:
1 hour**

**Cooking time:
40 minutes**

For a shortcut version of this delicious cake, just add unsweetened cocoa powder to an angel cake mix. Prepare the cake mix according to the package directions, *except* sift ⅓ cup cocoa powder and stir it into the dry ingredients for a one-step angel cake mix or into the flour ingredients for a two-step mix.

1½ cups egg whites (10 to 12 large eggs)

1 cup sifted cake flour or sifted all-purpose flour

1½ cups sifted powdered sugar

3 tablespoons unsweetened cocoa powder

½ teaspoon ground cinnamon

1½ teaspoons cream of tartar

1 teaspoon vanilla

1 cup sugar

Frozen Fruit Yogurt (see recipe, page 83) or purchased frozen peach yogurt

Sliced nectarines or sliced peeled peaches

Chocolate Sauce (see tip, above)

- Place egg whites in large mixing bowl and let stand at room temperature for 30 minutes.

- Meanwhile, sift together flour, powdered sugar, cocoa powder, and cinnamon three times. Set aside.

- Beat egg whites, cream of tartar, and vanilla with an electric mixer on medium speed until soft peaks form (tips curl). Gradually add the sugar, *2 tablespoons* at a time, beating on high speed until stiff peaks form (tips stand straight). Transfer to a larger bowl, if necessary.

- Sift about *one-fourth* of the flour mixture over the beaten egg whites; fold in gently. Repeat three more times to fold in remaining flour mixture.

- Pour into an ungreased 10-inch tube pan. Bake on the lowest rack in a 350° oven for 40 to 45 minutes or until the top springs back when lightly touched.

- *Immediately* invert cake (leave in pan); cool thoroughly. Loosen sides of cake from pan; remove cake. Cool completely. Serve cake with frozen yogurt, nectarines, and Chocolate Sauce. Garnish with mint leaves, if desired. Makes 16 servings.

Apple Cake

Per serving:
139 cal. (24% from fat), 2 g pro., 26 g carbo., 4 g fat,
0 mg cholesterol, 2 g dietary fiber, 89 mg sodium.

Preparation time:
15 minutes

Baking time:
25 minutes

The whole wheat flour, the oat bran, and the peel on the apples give this cake extra fiber. Using egg whites instead of whole eggs helps keep the fat and cholesterol in check.

Nonstick spray coating

⅔ cup sugar

½ cup packed brown sugar

¼ cup cooking oil

3 egg whites

⅔ cup all-purpose flour

⅔ cup whole wheat flour

½ cup oat bran

1½ teaspoons baking soda

1 teaspoon ground cinnamon

¼ teaspoon ground allspice or nutmeg

3 cups shredded unpeeled apples

Powdered sugar (optional)

- Spray a 13x9x2-inch baking pan with nonstick coating; set aside.

- Combine sugar, brown sugar, oil, and egg whites in a large mixing bowl. Beat with a wooden spoon until well blended. Add all-purpose flour, whole wheat flour, oat bran, baking soda, cinnamon, and allspice or nutmeg; stir just until moistened. Stir in shredded apples. Pour batter into the prepared pan.

- Bake in a 350° oven for 25 to 30 minutes. Cool on a wire rack. If desired, sift powdered sugar over top of cake. Makes 16 servings.

Fruit Crisp

Per serving:
201 cal. (21% from fat), 3 g pro., 39 g carbo., 5 g fat,
5 mg cholesterol, 3 g dietary fiber, 54 mg sodium.

Preparation time:
20 minutes

Baking time:
40 minutes

Slightly more fruit, less margarine, and no nuts in the topping make this crisp lighter than the classic recipe. To top it off, serve it with ice milk instead of ice cream.

2 tablespoons sugar

¼ teaspoon ground cinnamon

4 cups sliced peeled cooking apples, pears, or peaches

¼ cup quick-cooking rolled oats

2 tablespoons all-purpose flour

1 tablespoon brown sugar

1 tablespoon margarine, melted

¼ teaspoon ground cinnamon

1 cup vanilla ice milk

- Combine sugar and ¼ teaspoon cinnamon in a small mixing bowl. Place the sliced apples, pears, or peaches in a 9-inch pie plate. Sprinkle the sugar-cinnamon mixture over fruit. Toss gently to coat. Cover; bake in a 375° oven for 25 minutes.

- Meanwhile, stir together oats, flour, brown sugar, margarine, and ¼ teaspoon cinnamon. Sprinkle over partially cooked fruit mixture. Return to the oven and bake, uncovered, 15 to 20 minutes more or until fruit is tender. Serve warm with ice milk. Makes 4 servings.

Blueberry Cobbler

Per serving:
252 cal. (19% from fat), 4 g pro., 48 g carbo., 5 g fat,
5 mg cholesterol, 2 g dietary fiber, 120 mg sodium.

Preparation time:
20 minutes

Baking time:
15 minutes

This deep-dish fruit dessert is lighter than traditional cobblers because it leaves out an egg and uses less fat and sugar in its biscuitlike topping.

3	tablespoons sugar
2	teaspoons cornstarch
¼	teaspoon finely shredded lemon peel
¼	cup water
2	cups fresh or frozen blueberries
⅔	cup all-purpose flour
1	tablespoon sugar
1	teaspoon baking powder
¼	teaspoon ground cinnamon
¼	cup skim milk
1	tablespoon cooking oil
1	cup vanilla ice milk, Whipped Topper (see tip, page 72), or skim milk

- For filling, combine the 3 tablespoons sugar, the cornstarch, and lemon peel in a medium saucepan. Stir in water. Stir in blueberries. Cook and stir until thickened and bubbly. Cook and stir 2 minutes more. Keep filling hot.

- For biscuit topping, combine flour, the 1 tablespoon sugar, the baking powder, and cinnamon in a medium mixing bowl. Add the ¼ cup milk and the cooking oil; stir just until moistened. Spoon the hot blueberry filling into a 9-inch pie plate. Immediately drop topping into 4 mounds over the hot filling. If desired, sprinkle with a little additional ground cinnamon.

- Bake in a 400° oven for 15 minutes or until a wooden toothpick inserted into topping comes out clean. Serve warm with a small scoop of ice milk, Whipped Topper, or skim milk. Makes 4 servings.

Raisin-Bread Pudding

Per serving:
120 cal. (20% from fat), 7 g pro., 18 g carbo., 3 g fat,
72 mg cholesterol, 0 g dietary fiber, 134 mg sodium.

Preparation time:
15 minutes

Baking time:
35 minutes

The raisin bread and honey make this bread pudding a cut above the rest. What's more, it's only 120 calories per serving.

	Nonstick spray coating
2	eggs
2	egg whites
1½	cups skim milk
2	tablespoons honey
1	teaspoon vanilla
4	slices raisin bread, cubed (3 cups)

- Spray an 8x1½-inch round baking dish or 1½-quart casserole with nonstick coating.

- Beat eggs and egg whites until foamy in a large mixing bowl. Beat in milk, honey, and vanilla. Stir in bread cubes. Pour into the prepared baking dish.

- Bake in a 325° oven for 35 to 40 minutes or until a knife inserted near the center comes out clean.

- To serve, spoon warm bread pudding into dessert dishes. Makes 6 servings.

Choose-a-Fruit Ice

Frozen Fruit Yogurt

Per serving:
132 cal. (6% from fat), 5 g pro., 27 g carbo., 1 g fat,
4 mg cholesterol, 0 g dietary fiber, 65 mg sodium.

Preparation time:
18 minutes

Cooling time:
1 hour

Freezing time:
30 minutes

Creamy and refreshing, this fruit bonanza is low enough in calories and fat that you can enjoy it often. For a treat, serve it in regular ice cream cones. Regular cones have only about 20 calories each and no fat.

1½ cups sugar

1 envelope unflavored gelatin

1 12-ounce can (1½ cups) evaporated skim milk

2 tablespoons vanilla

4 8-ounce cartons plain low-fat yogurt

1 cup coarsely mashed peeled peaches or one 8-ounce can crushed pineapple (juice pack), well drained

- Stir together the sugar and unflavored gelatin in a large saucepan. Stir in the evaporated milk. Cook and stir over medium heat until mixture almost boils and sugar dissolves. Remove from the heat. Cool about 1 hour. Stir in the vanilla.

- Place the yogurt in a bowl. Use a wire whisk to gradually stir the milk mixture into yogurt until well combined.

- Stir the mashed peaches or drained pineapple into the yogurt mixture.

- Freeze the mixture in a 4- or 5-quart ice cream freezer according to the manufacturer's directions. Makes 2 quarts or 16 (½-cup) servings.

Choose-a-Fruit Ice

Per serving:
65 cal. (1% from fat), 0 g pro., 17 g carbo., 0 g fat,
0 mg cholesterol, 1 g dietary fiber, 0 mg sodium.

Preparation time:
20 minutes

Freezing time:
10 hours

Standing time:
20 minutes

This delightful ice is the perfect ending to just about any meal any time of year. For freshness as well as economy, make it with in-season fruits such as strawberries in summer and oranges in winter.

⅓ cup sugar

1 cup warm water

1½ cups fresh or frozen unsweetened strawberries or raspberries (thawed if frozen) or 1½ cups fresh orange sections (5 to 7 medium oranges) or two 11-ounce cans mandarin orange sections, drained

2 tablespoons lemon juice

Fresh strawberries (optional)

Fresh mint (optional)

- Stir sugar into water until dissolved. Combine sugar mixture, desired fruit, and lemon juice in a blender container or food processor bowl. Cover and blend or process until mixture is nearly smooth. Pour into a 9x5x3-inch loaf pan. Cover and freeze for 4 to 5 hours or until almost firm.

- Transfer frozen mixture to a chilled large mixing bowl. Beat with an electric mixer on medium speed for 2 minutes or until fluffy. Return fruit mixture to loaf pan. Cover and freeze for 6 hours or until firm.

- Before serving, let the frozen mixture stand about 20 minutes at room temperature. To serve, use an ice-cream scoop to scrape along the ice to form a mound. If desired, garnish each serving with a fresh strawberry and a sprig of fresh mint. Makes 6 servings.

Apple Dumplings

Per serving:
292 cal. (27% from fat), 2 g pro., 52 g carbo., 9 g fat,
0 mg cholesterol, 3 g dietary fiber, 51 mg sodium.

Preparation time:
40 minutes

Baking time:
35 minutes

This recipe is designed so there's no pastry to wrap under the bottoms of the apples. This keeps the pastry crisp and helps cut calories and fat, too.

⅔ cup all-purpose flour

Dash salt

2 tablespoons shortening

3 to 4 tablespoons cold water

4 medium cooking apples, peeled and cored

Ground cinnamon

Skim milk

¼ cup sugar

2 teaspoons cornstarch

½ cup apple juice or apple cider

2 teaspoons vanilla

2 teaspoons margarine

- For pastry, stir together flour and salt in a small mixing bowl. Using a pastry blender, cut in shortening until pieces are the size of fine crumbs. Sprinkle *1 tablespoon* of the water over part of the mixture; gently toss with a fork. Push moistened dough to side of bowl. Repeat, using 1 tablespoon of the remaining water at a time, until all dough is moistened. Form dough into a ball, and divide ball into 4 equal portions. Roll each portion into a ⅛-inch-thick circle.

- Place apples in a 9x9x2-inch baking pan. Sprinkle apples lightly with ground cinnamon. Place one pastry round on top of each apple, pinching pastry to fit around, but not underneath, the apple. Brush pastry with a little skim milk, and sprinkle lightly with additional ground cinnamon.

- Bake in a 375° oven for 35 minutes or until apples are tender and pastry is browned.

- Meanwhile, for syrup, combine sugar and cornstarch in a small saucepan. Stir in apple juice or apple cider. Cook and stir until thickened and bubbly. Cook and stir 2 minutes more. Remove from heat, and stir in vanilla and margarine. Serve warm apple dumplings in dessert bowls with syrup spooned over top. Makes 4 servings.

Apple Rice Pudding

Per serving:
92 cal. (11% from fat), 4 g pro., 17 g carbo., 1 g fat,
1 mg cholesterol, 1 g dietary fiber, 132 mg sodium.

Preparation time:
10 minutes

Cooking time:
20 minutes

Chilling time:
2 hours

With only 11 percent calories from fat and 92 calories total, this dessert is one you can afford to splurge on often. If you like, serve it with a graham cracker on the side. Graham crackers are low in both fat and calories.

2 cups skim milk

½ teaspoon ground cinnamon

¼ teaspoon salt

Dash ground nutmeg

⅓ cup long-grain rice

1½ cups coarsely chopped apples

¼ cup frozen whipped nondairy dessert topping, thawed

- Combine milk, cinnamon, salt, and nutmeg in a heavy saucepan. Bring to boiling. Stir in *uncooked* rice. Cover and cook over low heat for 20 to 25 minutes or until most of the milk is absorbed; stir occasionally. (Mixture may appear curdled.) Stir in apples. Cool thoroughly.

- Fold dessert topping into rice mixture. Spoon into dessert dishes. Chill 2 to 24 hours. Makes 6 servings.

Fruit Sauce

Per serving:
125 cal. (3% from fat), 1 g pro., 31 g carbo., 0 g fat,
0 mg cholesterol, 2 g dietary fiber, 3 mg sodium.

Preparation time:
15 minutes

Cooking time:
7 minutes

Chilling time:
1 hour

This sauce tastes great with just about any combination of fruit. You also can use it as a topping for ice milk and frozen yogurt.

1	8-ounce can pineapple tidbits (juice pack)
⅔	cup orange juice
2	tablespoons sugar
1	tablespoon cornstarch
1	tablespoon orange liqueur (optional)
¼	teaspoon vanilla
⅛	teaspoon finely shredded lemon peel
1	nectarine, pitted and thinly sliced, or ¾ cup frozen unsweetened peach slices, thawed
1	kiwi fruit, peeled, halved lengthwise, and sliced
½	cup seedless red grapes, halved

• For sauce, combine *undrained* pineapple, orange juice, sugar, and cornstarch in a small saucepan. Cook and stir until thickened and bubbly. Cook and stir 2 minutes more. Remove from heat. Stir in liqueur (if desired), vanilla, and lemon peel. Cover surface with waxed paper and chill for at least 1 hour.

• Before serving, combine nectarine or peach slices, kiwi fruit, and grapes in a serving bowl. Pour sauce over fruit. Stir gently to coat. Makes 4 servings.

Peachy Cherry Sauce

Per serving:
108 cal. (12% from fat), 2 g pro., 23 g carbo., 2 g fat,
0 mg cholesterol, 2 g dietary fiber, 23 mg sodium.

Preparation time:
15 minutes

Cooking time:
15 minutes

This refreshing sauce is a real fat bargain. It's hard to believe that something so good for you can taste so delicious.

2	cups sliced peeled peaches or sliced nectarines or frozen unsweetened peach slices
1	cup pitted dark sweet cherries or frozen unsweetened pitted dark sweet cherries
¼	cup lower-calorie orange marmalade
¼	cup orange juice
2	teaspoons cornstarch
1	teaspoon margarine
¼	teaspoon ground cinnamon or cardamom
½	cup frozen vanilla yogurt or ice milk

• Thaw fruits, if frozen. Combine marmalade, orange juice, cornstarch, margarine, and cinnamon or cardamom in a medium saucepan. Cook and stir until thickened and bubbly. Stir in fresh or frozen peaches or fresh nectarines and cherries. Cover and cook over medium heat for 10 to 12 minutes or until fruits are just tender, stirring once. Cool the fruit mixture slightly.

• To serve, spoon sauce into dessert dishes. Top each serving with a small spoonful of frozen yogurt or ice milk. Makes 5 servings.

Apricot Custards

Per serving:
128 cal. (18% from fat), 6 g pro., 21 g carbo., 3 g fat,
108 mg cholesterol, 1 g dietary fiber, 67 mg sodium.

Preparation time:
15 minutes

Baking time:
30 minutes

Start these custards an hour before suppertime. That way, they'll be done baking about the time you sit down to eat and cooled to just the right eating temperature by dessert time.

1 16-ounce can unpeeled apricot halves (water pack), drained

2 beaten eggs

1 cup skim milk

2 tablespoons sugar

½ teaspoon vanilla

Several drops rum flavoring or almond extract

Ground cardamom or ground nutmeg

- Reserve four apricot halves for garnish. Chop the remaining apricot halves; drain well on paper towels.

- Place four 6-ounce custard cups in a shallow baking pan. Divide chopped apricots among custard cups.

- Combine egg, milk, sugar, vanilla, and flavoring. Pour mixture over fruit. Sprinkle with cardamom or nutmeg.

- Place baking pan on oven rack. Pour boiling water around custard cups in baking pan to a depth of 1 inch.

- Bake in a 325° oven for 30 to 35 minutes or until a knife inserted near the centers comes out clean. Remove cups from water. Cool slightly before serving. Garnish with the reserved apricots. Makes 4 servings.

Chocolate Dream Pie

Per serving:
196 cal. (18% from fat), 5 g pro., 37 g carbo., 4 g fat,
1 mg cholesterol, 1 g dietary fiber, 112 mg sodium.

Preparation time:
55 minutes

Baking time:
1¾ hours

Cooling time:
20 minutes

Chilling time:
2 hours

This irresistible dessert is truly a dream. It has a rich chocolate flavor yet only 18 percent calories from fat.

3 egg whites

1 teaspoon vanilla

¼ teaspoon cream of tartar

Dash salt

½ cup sugar

½ cup sugar

¼ cup cornstarch

¼ cup unsweetened cocoa powder

⅛ teaspoon salt

2½ cups skim milk

1½ teaspoons vanilla

1 4-ounce container frozen whipped dessert topping, thawed

- Place egg whites in a mixing bowl and let stand 30 minutes at room temperature.

- Cover a baking sheet with plain brown paper. Draw a 9-inch-diameter circle on the paper; set aside.

- Beat together egg whites, vanilla, cream of tartar, and dash of salt until soft peaks form (tips curl). Gradually add ½ cup sugar and beat until stiff peaks form (tips stand straight). Pipe meringue through a pastry tube onto the circle on the brown paper, building up the sides to form a shell. Bake in a 300° oven for 45 minutes. Turn off oven and let dry in oven, with door closed, for 1 hour. Cool thoroughly on a wire rack.

- Meanwhile, for filling, combine ½ cup sugar, the cornstarch, cocoa powder, and ⅛ teaspoon salt in a heavy saucepan. Stir in milk. Cook and stir over medium heat until thickened and bubbly. Cook and stir 2 minutes more. Remove from heat. Stir in vanilla. Cover surface with waxed paper. Cool slightly without stirring, about 20 minutes. Pour into cooled shell. Chill thoroughly, at least 2 hours. To serve, pipe or spoon thawed topping over filling. Makes 8 servings.

Heavenly Cheesecake

Per serving:
220 cal. (27% from fat), 11 g pro., 31 g carbo., 7 g fat,
17 mg cholesterol, 1 g dietary fiber, 197 mg sodium.

Preparation time:
30 minutes

Baking time:
1 hour

Cooling time:
1¾ hours

Chilling time:
4 hours

Because this cheesecake is lower in fat, the top may crack during baking. But spooning the fruit on top will hide any cracks.

¾ cup crushed graham crackers

2 tablespoons margarine, melted

1 8-ounce package light cream cheese (Neufchâtel), softened

1 15-ounce container nonfat or lower-fat ricotta cheese

1 8-ounce carton plain nonfat yogurt

1 cup sugar

2 tablespoons all-purpose flour

2 tablespoons lemon juice

1 tablespoon vanilla

6 or 7 egg whites (¾ cup) or ¾ cup (6 ounces) refrigerated or frozen egg product, thawed

2 kiwi fruit, peeled and sliced

½ cup sliced strawberries

¼ cup blueberries

- For crust, combine the crushed graham crackers and melted margarine in a small mixing bowl. Press mixture onto the bottom of a 9-inch springform pan. Bake in a 325° oven 5 minutes. Cool the crust.

- Combine cream cheese and ricotta cheese in a large mixing bowl. Beat with an electric mixer on medium speed until smooth. Add the yogurt, sugar, flour, lemon juice, and vanilla. Beat on low speed until combined. Add egg whites or egg product. Beat on low speed just until combined. Pour into crust. Place springform pan on a shallow baking pan in oven.

- Bake in a 325° oven 55 to 65 minutes or until center appears nearly set when gently shaken. Cool 15 minutes. Loosen cheesecake from the sides of the pan. Cool for 30 minutes more; remove sides of pan. Cool completely. Cover and chill cheesecake 4 to 24 hours. Before serving, top cheesecake with kiwi fruit, strawberries, and blueberries. Makes 12 servings.

What's in an Egg

It used to be that eggs were severely limited in a low-fat, low-cholesterol diet, but researchers have taken another look at the egg. They now report that one egg contains 210 milligrams of cholesterol and 5 grams of fat—all located in the egg yolk. This cholesterol figure is considerably less than the 270 milligrams formerly listed. As a result, nutritionists say you can eat up to four egg yolks per week, unless your doctor has recommended otherwise. This includes not only the yolks you eat in egg dishes, but also those you use in other recipes.

If you want to reduce the cholesterol and fat in the egg dishes you make, substitute two egg whites for one whole egg in breakfast egg dishes, pancakes, and quick breads. And when adding hard-cooked eggs to breakfast dishes or salads, discard the yolks and use only the whites.

Fat and Calories Chart

Keep track of the fat and calories in the foods you eat with this handy chart. If the amount of fat is more than 0 but less than ½ gram it is listed as a trace (tr).

FOOD ITEM	Fat (g)	Cal.
ALFALFA SPROUTS; ¼ cup	tr	3
ANGEL FOOD CAKE, from a mix; ⅟₁₂ cake	tr	125
APPLES		
Dried; 1½-inch ring	tr	16
Fresh; 1 medium	tr	80
Juice, canned; ½ cup	tr	60
APPLESAUCE		
Canned, sweetened; ½ cup	tr	98
Canned, unsweetened; ½ cup	tr	53
APRICOTS		
Canned, juice-pack; ½ cup	tr	60
Canned, syrup-pack; ½ cup	tr	107
Dried; 1 half	tr	8
Fresh; 1 medium	tr	17
Nectar; ½ cup	tr	71
ARTICHOKES, cooked		
Fresh; 1 medium	tr	60
Hearts, frozen; ½ cup	tr	38
ASPARAGUS, cooked; ½ cup	tr	23
AVOCADO		
California; 6 ounces	30	300
Florida; 11 ounces	28	349
BACON		
Canadian-style; 1-ounce slice	2	52
Cooked, drained; 1 slice	3	36
BAGEL, plain; 1 (3½-inch-diameter)	1	180
BANANA; 1 medium	1	105
BARBECUE SAUCE, bottled; 1 tablespoon	tr	10
BARLEY, PEARL, cooked; ¾ cup	1	145
BEANS		
Cooked from dried (kidney, navy, pinto, lima); ½ cup	1	120
Green fresh, cooked; ½ cup	tr	22
Kidney, canned, drained; ½ cup	tr	108
Lima, large, frozen, cooked; ½ cup	tr	85
Pork and beans with sauce, canned; ½ cup	2	141
BEAN SPROUTS, fresh; ½ cup	tr	16

FOOD ITEM	Fat (g)	Cal.
BEEF, cooked, lean only		
Arm pot roast; 3 ounces	8	183
Flank steak; 3 ounces	9	175
Ground, 85% lean; 3 ounces	12	204
Ground, 90% lean; 3 ounces	7	162
Rib roast; 3 ounces	8	172
Round steak; 3 ounces	4	153
Sirloin steak; 3 ounces	6	165
Tenderloin; 3 ounces	8	174
BEETS, cooked, sliced; ½ cup	tr	26
BEVERAGES, alcoholic		
Beer, light; 12 ounces	0	96
Beer, regular; 12 ounces	0	140
Gin, rum, vodka, or whiskey; 1 ounce	0	71
Wine, dry white; 4 ounces	0	75
Wine, red; 4 ounces	0	82
BEVERAGES, nonalcoholic (see also Cocoa, Coffee)		
Club soda; 12 ounces	0	0
Cola, diet; 12 ounces	0	2
Cola, regular; 12 ounces	0	139
Lemon-lime, diet; 12 ounces	0	4
Lemon-lime, regular; 12 ounces	0	138
BISCUITS, baking powder, home recipe; 1 (2½-inch-diameter)	11	195
BLACKBERRIES, fresh or frozen; ½ cup	tr	37
BLACK-EYED PEAS		
Cooked from dried; ½ cup	tr	99
BLUEBERRIES, fresh or frozen; ½ cup	tr	41
BOLOGNA; 4½-inch-diameter slice	8	89
BREADS (see also Bagel, Croissant, Doughnuts, Pita Pocket Bread, Sweet Rolls)		
Breadstick, salted; 6½x1¼ inch	1	106
Crumbs, fine dry; ¼ cup	1	98
Crumbs, soft; ¼ cup	tr	30
French; 1 slice	1	100
Italian; 1 slice	tr	83
Mixed grain; 1 slice	1	65
Pumpernickel; 1 slice	1	80
Raisin; 1 slice	1	68
Rye; 1 slice	1	65
Sourdough; 1 slice	1	88
White, firm crumb; 1 slice	1	88
White, hamburger bun; 1 bun	2	129
White, hard roll; 1 roll	2	155
White, hot dog bun; 1 bun	2	115

FOOD ITEM	Fat (g)	Cal.
BREADS *(Continued)*		
White, soft crumb; 1 slice	1	75
Whole wheat; 1 slice	1	60
BROCCOLI, cooked; ½ cup	tr	22
BRUSSELS SPROUTS, cooked; ½ cup	tr	30
BUTTER; 1 tablespoon	12	102
BUTTERMILK; 1 cup	2	100
CABBAGE, raw, shredded; ½ cup	tr	8
CAKES, frosted 2-layer, from a mix (see also Angel Food Cake)		
Chocolate; ¹⁄₁₂ cake	11	313
White; ¹⁄₁₂ cake	16	387
Yellow; ¹⁄₁₂ cake	10	313
CANDY		
Candy-coated milk-chocolate pieces; 2 tablespoons	6	140
Caramels; 1 ounce (3 or 4)	3	115
Chocolate-covered peanuts; ¼ cup	18	238
Chocolate-covered raisins; ¼ cup	4	183
English toffee; 1 ounce	17	195
Fudge (chocolate with nuts); 1-inch square	5	114
Gumdrops; ¼ cup	tr	147
Hard; 1 ounce	0	109
Jelly beans; ¼ cup	tr	156
Milk chocolate; 1 ounce	9	145
Peanut brittle; 1 ounce	6	144
CARROTS, raw; 1 medium	tr	31
CATSUP; 1 tablespoon	tr	16
CAULIFLOWER, cooked; ½ cup	tr	15
CELERY, raw; ½ cup chopped	tr	10
CEREALS (approximately 1 ounce)		
Bran flakes; ⅔ cup	tr	84
Cornflakes; 1¼ cups	tr	110
Crisp-rice cereal; 1 cup	tr	112
Granola; ¼ cup	5	126
Puffed rice; 2¼ cups	tr	124
Puffed wheat; 2¼ cups	tr	99
Shredded wheat biscuits, small; ⅔ cup	1	103
Wheat flakes; 1 cup	1	110
CHEESECAKE, with graham cracker crust, home recipe, 8- or 9-inch cake; ¹⁄₁₂	32	447

FOOD ITEM	Fat (g)	Cal.
CHEESES		
American; 1 ounce	9	106
American cheese spread; 1 ounce	6	82
Blue; 1 ounce	8	100
Cheddar; 1 ounce	9	114
Cheddar, reduced-fat; 1 ounce	6	90
Colby; 1 ounce	9	112
Cottage, cream-style, 4% fat; ½ cup	5	109
Cottage, low-fat, 2%; ½ cup	2	102
Cottage, low-fat, 1%; ½ cup	1	82
Cream cheese; 1 ounce	10	99
Cream cheese, light; 1 ounce	5	60
Feta; 1 ounce	6	75
Monterey Jack; 1 ounce	9	106
Mozzarella, part skim milk; 1 ounce	5	72
Neufchâtel; 1 ounce	7	74
Parmesan, grated; 1 tablespoon	2	23
Ricotta, part skim milk; ½ cup	10	170
Ricotta, whole milk; ½ cup	16	214
Swiss; 1 ounce	8	107
CHERRIES		
Sweet, fresh; 1 cup	1	104
Tart, canned, water-pack; ½ cup	tr	45
CHICKEN BROTH, canned; ½ cup	1	19
CHICKEN, cooked		
Boneless, dark meat, no skin; 3 ounces	8	174
Boneless, white meat, no skin; 3 ounces	4	147
CHOCOLATE		
Milk chocolate; 1 ounce	9	145
Semisweet baking; 1 ounce	10	143
Semisweet chocolate pieces; ¼ cup	15	215
Sweet baking; 1 ounce	10	140
Unsweetened baking; 1 ounce	15	145
CHOCOLATE-FLAVORED SYRUP; 1 tablespoon	tr	43
CHOW MEIN NOODLES; ½ cup	7	118
CLAMS, canned, drained; 3 ounces	2	125
COCOA		
Beverage, with whole milk; 6 ounces	6	148
Unsweetened cocoa powder; 1 tablespoon	1	14
COCONUT, flaked, sweetened; ½ cup	12	170
COFFEE, brewed; ¾ cup	tr	2

FOOD ITEM	Fat (g)	Cal.
COOKIES		
Brownies with nuts,		
home recipe; 1 (2-inch square)	6	95
Chocolate chip, home recipe;		
1 (2-inch-diameter)	5	93
Coconut macaroon; 1 (2-inch-diameter)	6	109
Cream sandwich, chocolate;		
1 (1¾-inch-diameter)	2	50
Oatmeal, with raisins; 1 (2-inch-diameter)	3	61
Peanut butter, home recipe;		
1 (2-inch-diameter)	5	92
Sugar; 1 (2-inch-diameter)	3	59
Vanilla wafer; 1 (1¾-inch-diameter)	1	19
CORN		
Cream-style, canned; ½ cup	1	93
Ear, cooked; 1 (5-inch)	1	83
Whole kernel, frozen, cooked; ½ cup	tr	67
CORN BREAD, home recipe;		
1 (3-inch square)	8	203
CORN CHIPS; 1 cup (1⅓ ounces)	12	206
CORNED BEEF		
Brisket, cooked; 3 ounces	16	213
Packaged, thinly sliced; 3 ounces	6	118
CRAB-FLAVORED FISH		
(surimi seafood); 3 ounces	tr	82
CRABMEAT		
Canned, drained; 3 ounces	1	84
Cooked; 3 ounces	2	79
CRACKERS		
Rich round; 1 (1½-inch-diameter)	1	15
Saltine; 2 (2-inch squares)	1	25
Shredded wheat wafers; 1 (2-inch square)	1	21
Wheat wafers; 2 (1-inch squares)	1	18
CREAM		
Light; 1 tablespoon	3	29
Whipping (unwhipped); ½ cup	44	411
Whipping (whipped); ½ cup	22	205
CROISSANT; 1	12	235
CUCUMBER; 1 medium	tr	39
DATE, fresh or dried, pitted; 1	tr	23
DESSERT TOPPING		
Frozen, whipped, nondairy; 1 tablespoon	1	15

FOOD ITEM	Fat (g)	Cal.
DOUGHNUTS		
Cake; 1 (3¼-inch)	12	210
Raised; 1 (3¾-inch)	13	235
DUCK, cooked, meat only; 3 ounces	10	171
EGGNOG; ½ cup	10	171
EGGPLANT, peeled, cubed, cooked; ½ cup	tr	22
EGGS		
White; 1 large	0	17
Whole; 1 large	5	75
Yolk; 1 large	5	59
EGG SUBSTITUTE, frozen; 2 tablespoons	3	48
ENGLISH MUFFIN, whole; 1 (3½-inch)	1	140
FISH		
Breaded fish sticks, packaged,		
frozen, heated; 3 ounces	10	231
Catfish, baked or broiled; 3 ounces	5	132
Cod, baked or broiled; 3 ounces	1	89
Cod, batter-coated, fried; 3 ounces	9	169
Flounder or sole, baked or broiled; 3 ounces	2	99
Haddock, steamed; 3 ounces	1	98
Halibut, baked or broiled; 3 ounces	2	119
Orange roughy, baked or broiled; 3 ounces	8	143
Red snapper, baked or broiled; 3 ounces	1	109
Salmon, canned, drained; 3 ounces	6	130
Salmon, fresh, baked or broiled; 3 ounces	9	183
Sardines, canned in oil, drained; 3 ounces	10	177
Swordfish, baked or broiled; 3 ounces	4	127
Trout, whole dressed,		
baked or broiled; 3 ounces	5	164
Tuna, canned, oil-packed; 3 ounces	7	169
Tuna, canned, water-packed; 3 ounces	tr	111
Tuna, fresh, baked or broiled; 3 ounces	5	156
FLOURS		
All-purpose; ½ cup	1	228
Rye, medium; ½ cup	1	187
Self-rising; ½ cup	1	221
Whole wheat/graham; ½ cup	1	203
FRANKFURTERS/HOT DOGS (8 per pound)		
Beef; 1	17	184
Beef and pork; 1	17	183
Turkey; 1	11	129
GRAHAM CRACKER;		
1 (2½-inch square)	1	60

FOOD ITEM	Fat (g)	Cal.
GRAPEFRUIT		
Fresh; ½ medium	tr	39
Juice, unsweetened, canned; ½ cup	tr	47
GRAPES		
Fresh, seedless, green; 10 grapes	tr	35
Juice, unsweetened; ½ cup	tr	78
HAM, boneless, cooked, lean; 3 ounces	5	133
HOLLANDAISE SAUCE, from mix; 1 tablespoon	4	43
ICE CREAM TOPPINGS		
Caramel; 1 tablespoon	tr	52
Fudge; 1 tablespoon	3	64
Marshmallow creme; 1 tablespoon	0	53
ICE CREAM, vanilla		
Regular (10% fat); ½ cup	7	134
Rich (16% fat); ½ cup	12	175
Soft serve; ½ cup	11	189
ICE MILK, vanilla (4% fat); ½ cup	3	92
KIWI FRUIT; 1 medium	tr	46
LAMB, cooked		
Ground (shoulder); 3 ounces	12	239
Leg, lean; 3 ounces	7	163
Meat from loin chops, lean; 3 ounces	8	186
LENTILS, cooked; ½ cup	tr	115
LETTUCE, iceberg, shredded; ¾ cup	tr	5
LIVER, cooked		
Beef; 3 ounces	7	184
Chicken; 3 ounces	5	133
LOBSTER, broiled or grilled; 3 ounces	1	80
MARGARINE		
Diet; 1 tablespoon	6	49
Regular; 1 tablespoon	11	102
MARSHMALLOWS; 10 large or 1 cup tiny	0	180
MAYONNAISE		
Reduced-calorie (light); 1 tablespoon	5	50
Regular; 1 tablespoon	11	99
MELBA TOAST; 1 (1¾-inch-diameter)	tr	12

FOOD ITEM	Fat (g)	Cal.
MELONS		
Cantaloupe; ½ medium	1	94
Honeydew; ¼ medium	tr	113
Watermelon; 1 slice (1x10-inch-diameter)	2	152
MILK		
Chocolate drink (2%); 1 cup	5	180
Chocolate drink (whole); 1 cup	8	210
Evaporated, skim, undiluted; 1 cup	1	200
Evaporated, whole, undiluted; 1 cup	20	340
Instant nonfat dry, reconstituted; 1 cup	tr	85
1%; 1 cup	3	100
Skim; 1 cup	tr	86
Sweetened condensed, undiluted; 1 cup	27	982
2%; 1 cup	5	120
Whole; 1 cup	8	150
MUFFINS, baked from home recipes		
Blueberry; 1 (2½-inch)	7	177
Corn; 1 (2½-inch)	6	152
Oat bran; 1 (2½-inch)	7	171
MUSHROOMS		
Common, canned, drained; ½ cup	tr	19
Common, raw, sliced; ½ cup	tr	9
MUSTARDS		
Dijon; 1 tablespoon	3	24
Prepared; 1 tablespoon	1	12
NECTARINE; 1 medium	1	67
NUTS (see also Peanuts)		
Almonds, blanched, whole; ¼ cup	19	212
Cashews, dry-roasted, salted; ¼ cup	16	197
Hazelnuts (filberts), whole; ¼ cup	21	213
Macadamia nuts, oil-roasted, salted; ¼ cup	26	240
Mixed, dry-roasted, salted; ¼ cup	18	203
Mixed, oil-roasted, salted; ¼ cup	20	219
Pecans, halves; ¼ cup	18	180
Walnuts, halves; ¼ cup	16	160
OATMEAL, cooked; ¾ cup	2	109
OIL, cooking; 1 tablespoon	14	120
OLIVES		
Green, pitted and pimiento-stuffed; 5	3	24
Ripe (black), pitted; 5 large	2	26
ONION, chopped; ½ cup	tr	30
ORANGES		
Fresh; 1 medium	tr	60

Fat and Calories Chart *(continued)*

FOOD ITEM	Fat (g)	Cal.
ORANGES *(Continued)*		
Juice, fresh; ½ cup	tr	56
Juice, from frozen concentrate; ½ cup	tr	55
OYSTERS, shucked, cooked; 3 ounces	4	117
PANCAKES, home recipe; 1 (4-inch)	2	60
PASTAS, cooked		
Macaroni or spaghetti; ¾ cup	1	148
Noodles, egg; ¾ cup	2	160
PEACHES		
Canned, juice-pack; ½ cup	tr	55
Canned, syrup-pack; ½ cup	tr	95
Fresh; 1 medium	tr	37
PEANUT BUTTER		
Smooth or chunky; 1 tablespoon	8	95
PEANUTS		
Dry-roasted, salted; ¼ cup	18	206
Oil-roasted, salted; ¼ cup	18	209
PEARS		
Canned, juice-pack; ½ cup	tr	62
Canned, syrup-pack; ½ cup	tr	94
Fresh; 1 medium	1	98
PEAS		
Canned, drained; ½ cup	tr	59
Fresh, cooked; ½ cup	tr	67
Pods, cooked; ½ cup	tr	34
Split peas, cooked from dried; ½ cup	tr	116
PEPPERS		
Bell, chopped; ½ cup	tr	14
Green chili, canned, chopped, drained; ½ cup	tr	17
PICKLES		
Dill; 1 whole	tr	12
Sweet; 1 whole	tr	41
PIES; ⅛ of a 9-inch pie		
Apple	13	304
Cherry	13	308
Custard	10	220
Lemon meringue	11	266
Pecan	18	437
Pumpkin	12	275
PINEAPPLES		
Canned, chunks, tidbits, or crushed, juice-pack; ½ cup	tr	75

FOOD ITEM	Fat (g)	Cal.
PINEAPPLES *(Continued)*		
Canned, chunks, tidbits, or crushed, syrup-pack; ½ cup	tr	100
Fresh, chunks; ½ cup	tr	38
Juice, canned, unsweetened; ½ cup	tr	70
PITA POCKET BREAD;		
1 (6½-inch-diameter)	1	165
PIZZA, regular crust		
Cheese; ⅛ of a 15-inch pizza	9	290
Pepperoni; ⅛ of a 15-inch pizza	24	454
Sausage; ⅛ of a 15-inch pizza	16	381
PLUM, fresh; 1 medium	tr	36
POPCORN		
Plain, air-popped; 1 cup	tr	30
Plain, popped in oil, salted; 1 cup	3	55
PORK, cooked		
Boneless loin chop or roast, lean; 3 ounces	7	165
Country-style ribs, lean; 3 ounces	13	203
Shoulder, lean; 3 ounces	13	207
Tenderloin, breaded, fried; 3 ounces	13	277
Tenderloin, lean; 3 ounces	4	133
POTATOES		
Baked, with skin; about 7 ounces	tr	220
Boiled, peeled; about 5 ounces	tr	124
Chips; ½ ounce	5	74
French-fried (in vegetable oil); ½ cup	12	224
Frozen hash browns, cooked; ½ cup	9	170
Mashed with milk; ¾ cup	1	122
PRETZELS, thin sticks; 2 ounces	2	189
PUDDINGS, prepared from dry mix with whole milk		
Chocolate; ½ cup	4	150
Vanilla; ½ cup	4	145
RASPBERRIES, fresh; ½ cup	tr	30
REFRIED BEANS, canned; ½ cup	1	135
RICE (see also Wild Rice)		
Brown, cooked; ¾ cup	1	163
White, long-grain, cooked; ¾ cup	tr	198
White, quick-cooking, cooked; ¾ cup	tr	122
SALAD DRESSINGS		
Blue cheese; 1 tablespoon	8	77
Blue cheese, low-calorie; 1 tablespoon	2	30

FOOD ITEM	Fat (g)	Cal.

SALAD DRESSINGS (*Continued*)
Buttermilk/ranch; 1 tablespoon ......6........54
Buttermilk/ranch, low-calorie; 1 tablespoon ......0..........16
French; 1 tablespoon ......9........67
French, low-calorie; 1 tablespoon ......2........22
Italian, creamy; 1 tablespoon ......7........70
Italian, creamy, low-calorie; 1 tablespoon ......2........24
Italian, oil-based; 1 tablespoon ......9........69
Italian, oil-based, low-calorie; 1 tablespoon ......1........16
Mayonnaise-type; 1 tablespoon ......5........57
Thousand Island; 1 tablespoon ......6........59
Thousand Island, low-calorie; 1 tablespoon ......2........24

SALSA, chunky; 1 tablespoon ......tr........5

SAUSAGES
Bratwurst, cooked; 3 ounces ......24........275
Italian, cooked, links; 3 ounces ......22........274
Pepperoni, sliced; 1 ounce ......12........140
Polish, cooked; 3 ounces ......24........276
Pork, breakfast, cooked (16 per pound); 1 link ...4........48
Smoked links, cooked; 3 ounces ......26........286
Turkey, breakfast, cooked; 3 ounces ......13........195

SCALLOPS, steamed; 3 ounces ......1........96

SHERBETS; ½ cup ......2........135

SHORTENING, vegetable; 1 tablespoon ......13........113

SHRIMP
Batter-fried; 3 ounces ......11........195
Canned, drained; 3 ounces ......2........102
Fresh or frozen, cooked; 3 ounces ......1........84

SOUPS, canned, condensed
Cheese soup, with water; ¾ cup ......8........116
Chicken noodle, with water; ¾ cup ......2........56
Cream of mushroom, with water; ¾ cup ......7........98
Cream of mushroom, with whole milk; ¾ cup ...10........154
Cream of tomato, with water; ¾ cup ......1........65
Vegetable beef, with water; 1 cup ......1........59

SOUR CREAM
Dairy; 1 tablespoon ......3........31
Lower-calorie; 1 tablespoon ......1........15

SPINACH
Cooked; ½ cup ......tr........24
Fresh, torn; ¾ cup ......tr........9

SQUASH
Acorn, cooked, mashed; ½ cup ......tr........42
Zucchini, sliced, cooked; ½ cup ......tr........15

FOOD ITEM	Fat (g)	Cal.

STRAWBERRIES
Fresh, unsweetened; ½ cup ......tr........23
Frozen, sweetened, thawed; ½ cup ......tr........123

STUFFING MIXES, prepared;
Herb-seasoned; ½ cup ......9........215
Corn-bread; ½ cup ......9........215

SUGARS
Brown, packed; 1 tablespoon ......0........51
Granulated; 1 tablespoon ......0........48
Powdered, sifted; 1 tablespoon ......0........24

SWEET POTATOES, baked; 1 medium ......tr........118

SWEET ROLLS
Cinnamon; 1 (2½-inch square) ......6........179

TARTAR SAUCE; 1 tablespoon ......8........74

TOMATOES
Canned; ½ cup ......tr........24
Cherry; 1 ......tr........3
Fresh; 1 medium ......tr........26
Juice, canned; ½ cup ......tr........21
Sauce; ½ cup ......tr........37
Stewed; ½ cup ......tr........34

TORTILLA CHIPS; 10 (⅔ ounce) ......5........93

TORTILLAS
Corn; 1 (6-inch) ......1........61
Flour; 1 (8-inch) ......3........105

TURKEY
Breast meat, cooked, no skin; 3 ounces ......3........133
Breast meat, cooked, with skin; 3 ounces ......7........168
Dark meat, cooked, no skin; 3 ounces ......6........159
Dark meat, cooked, with skin; 3 ounces ......10........188
Ground, cooked; 3 ounces ......12........210

VEAL, boneless round, cooked, lean; 3 ounces ......3........127

WAFFLES, frozen; 1 (4-inch square) ......3........98

WILD RICE; ¾ cup ......tr........125

YOGURT
Fruit- or vanilla-flavored, frozen; ½ cup ......2........120
Fruit- or vanilla-flavored, low-fat; ½ cup ......1........116
Fruit- or vanilla-flavored, nonfat; ½ cup ......tr........75
Plain, low-fat; ½ cup ......2........72
Plain, nonfat; ½ cup ......tr........64

Index

95

Index (continued)